The Gatekeeper

TERRY EAGLETON

The Gatekeeper

A MEMOIR

St. Martin's Press ❧ New York

www.stmartins.com

ISBN 0-312-29122-1

First published in Great Britain by the Penguin Group

First U.S. Edition: July 2002

10 9 8 7 6 5 4 3 2 1

In memory of Norman Feltes

Contents

1

Lifers

The convent was a squat, ramshackle building, its roof more corrugated iron than Gothic pinnacle. It was set among high walls spiked with shards of glass, forbidding enough to repel voyeurs, religious obsessives, nun-stalkers, sex offenders, militant Protestants, enraged atheists. But the walls were also there to keep the occupants in. For this was a convent of enclosed Carmelite nuns, who once the gate had slammed behind them would see nobody but their fellow nuns and a few priests and altar boys for the rest of their lives.

I was the gatekeeper. As a ten-year-old altar server in the convent chapel, I had to be on hand when a novice, perhaps nineteen or twenty-one years old, took the veil and disappeared into the place for good. She would first be dressed as a bride to symbolize her marriage to Christ, her hair cropped almost to a crew-cut beneath the white lacy veil. In some cases, no doubt, the honeymoon would prove something of a disappointment. Then she would be ushered away by her fellow nuns to return decked in the black veil and rough brown habit of the Carmelite order. I heard later of a young woman who had turned down the Carmelites and opted instead for a religious order which allowed you to wear Marks & Spencer knickers. Though I myself had no personal acquaintance with the knickers of Carmelite nuns, I feel sure that they were forbidding, skin-chafing affairs, slid into place with steel bolts, as the order never missed even the mildest chance for mortification.

The bishop, an old codger from Kildare with the walk of a navvy and the face of a wino, would arrive to officiate at the ceremony. One of us altar boys would be appointed to carry his mitre, the high plush hat he wore on such occasions, while another boy would bear his crosier or symbolic golden staff. We would hold these props through white silken bands draped around our shoulders, the grubby fingers of boyhood being judged too profane. The bishop would require this stuff at various particularly sacred moments in the proceedings, and since these moments were hard to predict we would be on watch for our cue from the master of ceremonies, who had to be deft enough to help the bishop on with his hat without knocking off his skullcap.

We had to look sharp, since at one such clothing a minuscule altar boy, bewildered by the MC's impatient gestures to his temples, threw the last vestiges of secular rationality to the winds and ended up solemnly placing the richly embroidered mitre on his own head, in a surreal parody of the proceedings. The boy with the crosier had the ticklish task of handing the bishop this ornate, outsize version of a shepherd's crook while simultaneously going down on one knee and kissing the Episcopal ring. Later in life, describing this piece of acrobatics to some agnostic friends, I realized from their ribald laughter that the phrase 'going down to kiss the bishop's ring' had a rather more salacious meaning than had occurred to me at the age of ten.

Once the *Te Deum* had been sung and the ceremony was ended, the newly clothed sister would be on hand in the convent parlour to say a last goodbye to her family. The parlour, a kind of no man's land or air-lock between the nuns' enclosure and the outside world, was a completely bare room bisected from floor to ceiling by a black iron grille. There were closed doors behind the grille on the nuns' side, and symbolic spikes jutted ominously from it at the visitor. The nuns' side of the parlour connected with the intricate bowels of the convent, while the other side opened through a double door on to the outside world. Both these external doors had to be closed before the door behind the grille could be opened, one of the many arcane rules of the house.

It was my job on these occasions to conduct the young woman's parents into the parlour to see their daughter for the last time. They would kneel shyly on the profane side of the grille, partly out of piety and partly because there was nowhere to sit, while their newly-wed daughter knelt smiling on the holy side, her veil thrown back, chaperoned by a kneeling reverend mother whose veil would be lowered. Catholicism seemed to be mainly a matter of kneeling. There was a touch of the zoo about the scene, as though the young creature behind the bars was some exotic, well-nigh extinct species, the reverend mother was her proud keeper and her parents a couple of venerating animal enthusiasts. Then, after a few shambling, perfunctory words had passed between parents and child, the reverend mother would nod discreetly to me, like an officer giving the go-ahead to an execution squad, and I would hold the door of the parlour open for the mother and father to leave, shutting their daughter from their sight for ever as they groped their way sniffling from the room like a couple of blind beggars. Somebody had to do the shit jobs.

For all its drab outer appearance, the convent was Gothic enough in its own way. It was really two separate spaces hinged cunningly together: the sealed interior of the nuns' quarters, and then, outside the enclosure, a few public rooms, a small chapel open to local people, and the lay sisters' dingy apartments. These two spaces met in a kind of faultline of turntables, concealed doors, secret compartments, small cupboards accessible from both sides, so that the whole building was a sort of *trompe l'œil*, like a crazy house at a fairground or an Escher drawing. It was as though the familiar world could open at any moment on to an alternative universe, only inches away from it yet incomparably remote. It seemed a reasonable image of the religious life.

It was also an image of my fissured life as a child. One moment I would be playing tag outside the corner shop, and the next moment I would slip through a black hole into a realm unimaginably remote, where my Protestant friends could not follow and where secular reason slithered to an abrupt halt. The convent was both drab and outlandish, mundane and full of mystery, as the odour of incense mixed with the smell of cabbage water and young women with flat Mancunian accents, whose real names were perhaps Mary O'Connor and Agnes Byrne but who were now Sister Teresa Maria of the Holy Cross or Sister Francis Josepha of the Little Flower, slept on wooden planks, rose before dawn to pray and were constantly hungry.

That the place was set on the fringes of Manchester made it seem even more bizarre, as though one were to stumble on a genuine moated castle in the middle of Memphis. There were drawers which slid noiselessly inwards when pulled from behind a wall, turntables which spun spookily without apparent human agency, and the eyes of immured virgins observing you through one-way screens. The drawers and turntables were to be found mostly in the sacristy, another place of passage between inner and outer worlds. Here the priest and altar servers donned their robes for Mass, while the sister sacristan, spectrally concealed on her side of the wall, placed vessels for the Mass in a drawer which would slide suddenly open like something in an inept horror movie. One or two of the more roguish priests would amuse the altar boys by feigning terror when the drawer shot out, pulling imaginary pistols or staging grotesque coronaries.

There was also a turntable in the wall for larger items to be passed in and out of the enclosure, and from time to time this would include the convent watchdog, Timothy. Watchdogs are as necessary to convents as wimples. Sometimes I had to lug Timothy on to the turntable so that he could be taken into the enclosure, as though required for some secret bestial rite. I would hear the sister sacristan murmur 'Deo gratias, Terry' through the wall, which was really a holy way of saying 'Hi', to which I would reply, 'Deo gratias, sister, Timothy is coming in now.' Then I would heave the dog on to the splintered wooden turntable and crank him round from my side while she tugged away from hers. He would disappear from sight, lugubrious and rheumy-eyed, the only male creature ever to penetrate the enclosure. Perhaps they blindfolded him when he reached the other side. Once or twice I had to repress a mad urge to leap on to the turntable myself, hands lolling and tongue drooping, growling and slavering as I was hauled in.

One whole wall of the chapel sanctuary was another grille with more symbolic spikes, and from behind this the sisters heard Mass through a one-way screen of faded black cloth. This meant that they could see the altar servers as we pottered around the altar; in fact we were the only males, however mildly so, they ever saw. They did not regard the priest as a man. We, however, could not see them. Or at least I saw only their mouths, when they received communion. I would stand beside the priest at a small hatch in the grille, and as one mouth after another presented itself fleetingly in this dark space I would hold the heavy silver communion plate beneath it like a solid napkin, ready to catch any sacred host that fell. After a time I became as familiar with these thirty or so mouths, some puckered and sparse-toothed, others moist and well-furnished, as I was with the letters of the alphabet.

None of the mouths seemed adorned by a beard, which struck me as strange. For I was convinced that there was a ginger-bearded nun in the place, having caught an appalling glimpse of her on one of the rare occasions when I was allowed into the courtyard leading to the enclosure. An elderly nun was sick, and I accompanied the priest as he took the blessed sacrament to her, swinging a thurible or carrying a lighted candle, I can't remember which. There were two large garage-like doors which led into the depths of the convent, and as the priest and I approached them they glided mysteriously open from the inside, as gates sometimes did in the movies. As we passed inside them, I could not resist the Lot's-wife-like temptation to turn and look at whoever was behind one of the doors. I saw, or thought I saw, a plump, middle-aged nun with the standard-issue peaches-and-cream complexion, but with coarse, hog-like ginger bristles sprouting from her chin. Maybe this moment of hermaphroditic horror is a false memory, or maybe not: if a nun did have facial hair, it would have been a sinful act of vanity for her to pluck it out.

The only time I actually spoke to a nun was when Sister Angela taught me the Latin I needed to serve Mass. I would meet her for an hour a week in the parlour, she kneeling on her side of the grille and I kneeling on mine, and her veil would be lifted since I was only eight or nine years old. Had pubescence suddenly seized me like a fit of the shakes, cracking my treble and pimpling my cheeks, the veil would have clamped down like a safety curtain. Once I had hair on my own chin, I was no longer allowed to see the hair on theirs. Mother Angela had the regulation-issue flat Mancunian accent and peaches-and-cream complexion, like a cross between *Coronation Street* and *The Sound of Music*. She was shrewd, forthright, and I suspect, in some other life altogether, a good laugh. Years later, when I had some reputation as a leftist theologian, I came back to see her, and despite my undeniable post-pubescence she lifted her veil. But this was because the Catholic Church was now awash with a tide of reform which was lapping up even against this outpost of ascetic traditionalism. She greeted me with her usual dry friendliness, but expressed the hope that I was not '*too* radical', though I am sure she knew that I was. The pale-faced urchin whose pronunciation of '*laetificat*' she had gently corrected was buried for ever beneath a truculent intellectual with a Julius Caesar haircut. At this turbulent time, all the religious orders were struggling to recruit and losing members hand over fist, as monks and nuns hopped one after another over the glass-spiked walls to find spouses, jobs in social work and Marks & Spencer knickers. It was like an ecclesiastical version of *Escape from Colditz*.

There were two lay sisters in the convent, one dumpy, deaf and sardonic and the other asthmatic, obsequious and permanently flustered, who did the shopping, ran the errands and acted generally as a link between inside and outside worlds. Otherwise, the nuns were linked to the outside world only by the sun and rain. The enclosed sisters would have had no idea who the prime minister was or what a television set looked like, since they read no newspapers except a papist rag modestly entitled *The Universe*. (It is said of the Catholic author Hilaire Belloc that he once obtained admission as a press correspondent to a high-level conference by loftily informing the doorman that he represented the Universe.) If a clutch of atomic bombs had laid waste Europe, the nuns would have known nothing of it until the fall-out began to drift their way. Indeed, some of them would never have heard of atomic bombs or Elvis Presley or washing-up liquid, used a telephone or been aware that India was no longer part of the British empire. What limited truck with the secular world they needed to survive was delegated to the lay sisters. My mother, who was a kind of convent groupie, was assured by one of these sisters that when she arrived in heaven, the two sons whom she had lost as infants would come to her as grown men. Even my pious mother saw fit to wonder how she had come by this remarkable piece of information.

My father sometimes did odd jobs around the convent, and once dashed into the sanctuary during Mass when a candle keeled over and set an altar cloth alight. For a few dramatic moments he was in full view of the sisters behind their screen, no doubt the first male animal apart from Timothy and we altar boys that some of them had clapped eyes on for thirty years. As I have mentioned, they did not regard priests as men. Some of the senior altar servers did not quite regard themselves as men either, at least in the stereotypical sense of the word. There was a lantern-jawed Irishman with a mild touch of religious mania who always seemed reluctant to take off his vestments when Mass was over, and spent a little time admiring himself in the window before doffing his cassock with a sigh. There were, of course, no mirrors in the convent. The nuns were Dracula-like in their distaste for them.

One elderly nun was said to be afflicted with the stigmata, though 'afflicted' is perhaps too impious a word. Like most stigmatists, her anatomical knowledge seemed less than accurate, since she was said to bear the marks of Christ's wounds in her palms, whereas crucifixion must surely have been through the wrists. I have no doubt that a convent full of permanently immured celibates can breed the odd miracle, given the long-range psychical havoc that a single disturbed adolescent can wreak. The greatest miracle to its credit, however, was the reclaiming of Tom McCormack.

McCormack was an Irish navvy who lived close to the convent, and a notorious lapsed Catholic. Even in those pious days, being a lapsed Catholic was almost acceptable; it was rather like being a country rather than a city member of a club, still on the books but less in evidence around the joint. 'Lapsed Catholic' was a convenient label for ensuring that you never actually left the Church; it simply shifted you from one ontological category to another, rather like resigning your peerage but staying on in politics. In any case, it put you in some remarkably distinguished company. Better to burn with Graham Greene than share paradise with Bing Crosby.

McCormack had not been to Mass for years, and was a boozer to boot. One Christmas Eve, however, as midnight approached, he and his wife heard the convent bells tolling as they lay in bed. They were actually ringing for midnight Mass, a practice which had recently been reintroduced. But McCormack's wife concluded that the convent was on fire, and got her husband to dress and run down to help. He stumped down on his stiff leg to find the congregation filing dutifully into the chapel, and was greeted like the prodigal son by the enraptured lay sisters. Unable to back out, he stayed for Mass, and from then on ritually returned every Christmas. He did not, however, go to Mass on Sundays, no doubt judging this to be a little immoderate, as well as detrimental to his mildly louche status as a lapsed Catholic. His wife had had her own miracle some years before, when her son's ship had gone down in the Atlantic during the war, and she heard him calling to her. It seems a lot more credible than the Immaculate Conception.

People sometimes talk of the monastic life as escapist. Never to handle money is a privilege reserved for royalty and ascetics. But while not knowing that Europe has just been wiped off the map is a luxurious kind of ignorance, there is another sense in which being in a convent is about as escapist as being in Wormwood Scrubs. True escape would mean getting out, not staying in. The late-night drunk who once clambered over the Berlin wall from west to east in a fit of absent-mindedness was not trying to escape. The life of these young women was harder than a Victorian housemaid's. Most of them, no doubt, were too young when they signed up to have much to sacrifice in the first place; it was not as though they were abandoning rock-star boyfriends or glamorous careers as neurosurgeons. Most of them would have known scant comfort at home: the majority of English Catholics, then as now, were of Irish working-class stock rather than cronies of Evelyn Waugh. Their renunciation of the world was perhaps as much ignorance as courage; they could be free of it because they were already, like a teetotaller taking the pledge. Taking the veil was a way of quarantining oneself from occasions of sin, since a convent offers few opportunities for really spectacular vice.

It may be that the corridors of the place surged with lust and bile, strewn with the detritus of lesbian orgies and sour with the stench of spiked ambitions. Perhaps those ghostly turntables concealed murderous rivalries and libidinous rituals, unspeakable rites in which cockerels were drained of their blood and some plump young postulant was held down on the altar to have her gizzard slit, while her weird sisters blasphemously gabbled snatches of the Mass backwards in their cracked Northern voices. One kind of postmodernist would be interested only in whether they were having sex with each other. Even if they were not, there would certainly have been some bickering and bitchery, cussedness, sour temper and erotic entanglements, a whole complex micro-politics.

Even so, it is hard to organize genocide or refugee-running from a convent cell, or force Burmese children into slavery. These pious late adolescents did not take the veil because they abominated the world and abjured the flesh, since they knew too little of such things in the first place. The world from which they abdicated was mostly one they cherished, a place of parents and siblings, not of greed and exploitation. Only some obscure impulse of love could have driven them to this joyless existence, as tough as a goldminer's and as thankless as a bum-bailiff's. They rose to pray several times during the night, ate like birds, had no personal possessions, and needed enough forbearance to spend the rest of their days confined with a bunch of crankish others within the same bleak walls. It was rather like opting to be banged up in a broom cupboard by Hezbollah.

Most of them, then, were probably somewhere midway between martyrs and suicides. The martyr freely surrenders a life which is precious, whereas the suicide shucks off an existence which has become worthless. Suicide is also usually a private affair, whereas martyrdom is a kind of socializing of one's death, placing it at others' disposal so that, to adopt a phrase of Auden's, it may be modified in the guts of the living. Choosing to repudiate what you cherish may be foolish, but at least it is not suburban. These women deliberately threw their lives away, a gesture which requires the defiant absurdism of the Dadaist rather than the calculations of the actuary or the zeal of the do-gooder. In refusing the powers of this world, their existence became as pointless as a work of art. It is true that as 1950s women they would not have enjoyed much worldly power in the first place; but their lives as religious plucked a public point from this impotence, converted it to a collective symbol.

Timorously conservative as they were, like almost all English Catholics of their day, they would not have regarded the religious life as in the least political. Indeed, it was not, at least in any orthodox sense of the word, which was just what was political about it in a more subtle sense. They prayed for the conversion of Russia yet were communists themselves, who ritually avoided the first-person pronoun and spoke instead of 'our (reverend) mother', 'our dog', 'our dustbin'. No doubt they each owned a toothbrush, but they had no clothes of their own, not even underclothes, and no need of a comb. They believed fervently in wives being submissive to their husbands, and were radical separatists long before the phrase was invented. Their vows of poverty, celibacy and obedience left them as free from material encumbrances as a guerrilla fighter, who can ill afford to be hampered by a mortgage. There was plenty of common-or-garden, non-optional poverty in the area around them. It was my home town of Salford, which even today is rated the unhealthiest city in the United Kingdom, and which in those days could hardly boast a lower middle class, let alone an opera house. But by freely assuming what for others was a fatality, perversely choosing what for the rest of us was just to be endured, the nuns turned it into a symbolic statement, raised it to the second power. In living their own lives, they were saying something about ours. In divesting themselves of the world they were prefiguring their own deaths, dying every moment; so that the ultimate self-abandonment of death, which for the rest of us is a matter of coercion, would become in their case a kind of free act.

What was most subversive about them, however, was their implacable otherworldliness. There are tough-minded types who believe that this world is the best we can muster, some of whom are known as materialists and the rest as conservatives.

Whatever they call themselves, the hard-nosed realists who claim that there is no need for another world have clearly not been reading the newspapers. These women, by contrast, acknowledged in their own eccentric way the wretchedness of human history, which they would no doubt have called the sinfulness of the world, and were thus the reverse of the bright-eyed liberal modernizers.

Preposterous as it may seem in these pragmatic days, they clung to the quaintly outmoded view that there was too much cruelty and aggression in the world for it to be merely accidental, or solvable by piecemeal reform. They were thus freaks and deviants, at least from the standpoint of those moderate, reasonable folk who suspect that there is nothing much awry with the planet which a touch more mutual understanding, a spot of civil rights or a few more bags of grain might not patch up. Nothing could be more extravagantly idealist than such streetwise realism. It is rejected by most intelligent conservatives, though not for the same reasons it is spurned by the left. Like socialists and nuclear physicists, but unlike pragmatists and positivists, the nuns were never so parochial as to believe that what they saw around them was all there could ever be. For them, the flaw of the world ran so deep that it cried out for some thoroughgoing transformation, known in their jargon as redemption. Short of this, things were likely to get a lot worse.

Their view of human history, whatever one might say of their solutions to it, was thus entirely realistic. Inventories of carnage are usually suspect. But it was reckoned in 1970 that the number of humanly caused deaths in the twentieth century, by far the bloodiest of historical epochs, stood at about 100 million. Thirty years later, countless more mass-acres would need to be added to that figure. The story of humanity has been one unbroken din of hacking and goug-ing, as any history of the world will confirm. Few narratives are more grossly improbable. For the first few aeons, hardly anything of interest happens, and the characters are mere sketches for credible, well-rounded human beings. Then, as if desperate to sustain the reader's drifting attention, the author throws the last shreds of realism shamelessly to the winds, brazenly squeezing his storyline for every last drop of sensationalism. A dwarfish Corsican corporal conquers a large slice of the globe, while a demented Georgian peasant butchers millions of his own countryfolk. In a absurdly extravagant flight of fantasy, the joint wealth of the three richest men in the world is said to equal the combined wealth of 600 million of the poorest. A sickly sentimental twist of plot has no less than an implausible 200 babies in the world's poorest countries die every hour. As the fable lurches erratically towards its later stages, the last semblance of narrative unity shatters into a mish-mash of wars, famines, tyrannies and revolutions, with sub-plots left hanging care-lessly in mid-air, the same incidents mindlessly repeated, characters hastily recycled and potentially fruitful storylines casually aborted. Nobody would believe a word of it for a moment.

Certainly my Carmelites did not. In their own way they would have agreed with Henry Ford that history is bunk, which is why they were where they were. Not to escape from history; the convent was not a life-raft in a storm. But not to change it either; they could hardly reform a world they never set foot in. Their role was to symbolize the kind of drastic self-abandonment which the world would need if it were to become just. They were a sign not of what was to be done, but of how much it would take. And this, no doubt, is one reason why right-thinking liberals, along with a good many socialists, would think them a little over the top. So, no doubt, would some feminists, since self-sacrifice has traditionally been a woman's speciality. From this viewpoint, the only redeeming feature about these nuns was that they were not in the service of men. Or at least they were in the service of one man only, and he, being conveniently absent from earth, required no cooking, laundry or sexual comfort.

They did not, of course, believe that history was *just* bunk. That would have been an excessively Protestant point of view. Indeed, it would have been heretical. If humanity was beyond hope, why get up several times a night to pray for it? Raymond Williams, writing in his book *Modern Tragedy* of those for whom the death camps signal the blasphemy of all hope, declares this, too, to be a blasphemy in its way; for if there were those who built the camps, there were others who died trying to destroy them. Marx called history a nightmare, but he thought there had to be a way of dreaming it which might allow you to wake up. The worst nightmare, of course, is to think that you have woken up only to discover that you are still dreaming, and there are plenty of political examples of this. But if history was to be undone, it could only be from the inside. The Christian gospel invites us to contemplate the reality of human history in the broken body of an executed political criminal. The message this body proclaims, as the theologian Herbert McCabe puts it, is uncompromising: if you don't love you're dead, and if you do love you'll be killed.* Here, then, is the pie in the sky, the opium of the people, the sentimental twaddle of salvation.

I was to study tragedy later, at Cambridge. But by then I had already known one broken, despairing body.

This creed contrasts with the delusions of those who imagine that the future will be pretty much like the present, only rather more so. 'The present plus more options', as someone remarked of postmodern pluralism. Whether or not the future will be worse, it will certainly be hard to recognize. The seriously bizarre idealists, those with their heads buried most obdurately in the sands, are the hard-nosed fantasists who live their lives as though the IMF, Clint Eastwood movies and chocolate chip cookies will still be up and running in 3,000 years time. Compared to this crazed common sense, the hairiest, most wild-eyed apocalypticist looks like a tepid liberal. Equally science-fictional is the belief that capitalism will finally get round to feeding the world. If the political left had promulgated such a transparent absurd-ity for as long as its opponents have peddled this lie, it would have been howled down without mercy.

These Carmelites lived as though history could disappear down the plughole at any moment, which is the simple truth. But if it did, then it would find them with empty hands, bodies cleansed as far as possible of desire, and so would not catch them napping. They could pull a fast one on death by acting it out in their lives, performing their own demise and thus cheating it of its terrors. By being in but not of the world, their existence was a kind of irony; but in courting

* See Herbert McCabe OP, *God Matters* (London, 1987), especially Chapter 8.

one form of irony they needed to avoid another. They were not to strive to make life sweeter by political action or works of charity, since this would bind them to the very world they repudiated. Instead, their role was to bear witness to the passing away of that world, prefigure in their own lives the death of history, by proclaiming in eye-catchingly theatrical style how little really matters in the end. Their business was simply to take pity on the plight of humanity, and to intercede ceaselessly on its behalf. No anodyne whiff of social hope, no square-jawed ideology of progress, was to be allowed to obscure the truth of just how dire things were with us, and of just how much it would take to repair them.

Years later, I was to encounter a very different set of nuns. They were American sisters from various religious orders, 200 or so in all, and I was teaching them on an MA course near New York. It was the fag-end of the 60s, and the air was effervescent with insurgency. These were new-style nuns of distinctly non-penguin appearance, devotees of mascara and Che Guevara, full of psychotherapeutic wisdom and fatiguing American zest. There seemed nothing they did not find exhilaratingly positive, from a plug of matted hair in the sink to a rusty hubcap, and when we trooped off to Broadway to see *Hair*, with its ten seconds of furtive nudity, a few of them had to be restrained from climbing on stage and cavorting around. They could sense the Holy Spirit stirring in a corkscrew or a bag of chips. Unlike Sister Angela, they turned somersaults at Mass, and occasionally turned up at class dressed in the *New York Times* to highlight the importance of human communication. They sang a strange blend of Joan Baez and Gregorian plainchant and enjoyed Being Themselves.

They were not ascetics, but modish young women in lipstick and high heels who smoked and drank, as Americans still did in those days, and seemed to regard religion as a free form of psychotherapy. There was a Dutch psychiatrist teaching on the course, who made the disastrous misjudgement of allowing one of the nuns to consult him privately. Before the week was out there was a queue of them of Yankee stadium proportions outside his door. They submitted MA theses which consisted of video film of themselves in touch with Nature, scampering around the campus lawns in profanely tight shorts, running barefoot up tree-trunks or listening intently to what the grass was murmuring. I soon learned that it was not really done to refuse anyone the MA, since the sisters provided a lucrative source of income for the college. At Mass, an orgy of hugging and Dylanish croaking from which they reeled away tearful and semi-orgasmic, they filed up to the altar one by one and squirted wine into the chalice from a lemon squeezer, to demonstrate the sacredness of the commonplace. In place of more traditional religious greetings, they murmured slogans to each other like 'The bread is rising' or 'He's coming, He's coming!', which I took to be eschatological rather than erotic, and gave each other hamfisted versions of the Black Power salute.

We went to visit a Headstart programme for pre-school children in a deprived area of Manhattan, and one of the sisters took a black child on her knee and asked effusively for a needle and thread to mend a rip in his jeans. This seemed embarrassingly like trying to fix a busted rib with a band-aid, but the African-American running the programme wandered off instantly to fetch a sewing kit. It was more sensible to make use of these women than self-indulgently denounce their liberal delusions. They were hot for redemption, but lived in a Woodstock-like world where there was no need for it. Their government was meanwhile busy butchering the Vietnamese. Everyone seemed to feel comfortable in their bodies, except perhaps for the Vietnamese. One of the nuns wrote me a paper comparing *Coral Island* with *Lord of the Flies*, observing as she handed it to me that she had not actually been able to read *Coral Island*. Since knowledge in those days was oppressive and uncool, this made the essay well worth an A. Most of them probably went over the wall a few years later, and are now social workers or business executives. Since they believed in anti-élitist spirit that nobody should be different from anyone else, they ended up doing themselves out of a job, like those radical 60s professors who ought logically to have sat at the back of their own classes and barracked.

Some years later, I encountered a similar kind of culture when I was a visiting professor at San Diego. My first undergraduate class seemed to consist almost entirely of half-naked young people who had just wandered in off the beach. One or two of them seemed to be wearing flippers, and I caught sight of what looked suspiciously like a snorkel. There was a general air of wetsuits and surfboards. I delivered a robust, impassioned first lecture, which they seemed to appreciate in their sun-dazed, slit-eyed way. After class, one young man dressed only in a pair of vermilion-coloured knee-length trousers padded across to the podium and thanked me for the session. 'But d'ya know what, professor?' he said. 'You're trying too hard.' He went on to confide with touching concern for my welfare that most of his fellow students were either drunk or doped, and were really not worth the energy I was misguidedly lavishing on them.

These were heady times for Catholics. In the wake of the second Vatican Council, a surge of spiritual renewal had seized the Church. Bishops were mocked and heckled, while lay people clamoured to hear their own confessions and took to curing anyone they could lay their hands on, diseased or not. Priests who had kissed one another in private for decades began to do it in broad daylight. There were some startling overnight changes of personality, as aloof, ascetic monks suddenly reinvented themselves as raucous thigh-slapping Trotskyites or threw aside their habits for shaggy sweaters and bellbottomed trousers. Sometimes they would appear with one arm slung defiantly round a liberated nun decked out in a sack dress, beads and sandals, but still unmistakably clerical around the pink cheeks, sensible hair and cheerful countenance. The kiss of peace during Mass, when you would turn and embrace the stranger beside you, began to last so long that priests wondered whether to break it up by ringing a handbell.

Just as the Bolshevik artists had taken drama out of the élitist theatres into farms and factory yards, so Mass was now being celebrated in pubs, kitchens, car-parks, swimming-pools, perhaps even the occasional telephone box. Some enthusiasts wore wooden crosses around their necks so cumbersome that it was hard to know whether they were practical or ornamental. Young men foamed brownly at the mouth during Mass, while downtrodden housewives who had previously been heard to say little except 'Your dinner's getting cold' began babbling deliriously in tongues. It sounded to the sceptical ear suspiciously like a garbled version of Home Counties English. Everywhere people were meditating, levitating, joyfully masturbating. Nobody was making dogmatic moral judgements any more. One liberal-minded bishop, asked in public how he would judge a couple engaged in extra-marital sex, replied that rather than condemn them from some lofty vantage-point he would like to 'get alongside them'. A fellow prelate, faced with a similar query, responded that he would like to 'expose himself to them'. The English Catholic Church's leading theologian, gradually persuaded that the Church was about as charitable an institution as San Quentin, threw it all up in disgust and ran off with a woman called Florence. 'Pope to Visit Florence' threatened the headline of the papist press, but it turned out to mean the city. While students were organizing sit-ins, progressive Christians were staging pray-ins.

Catholics who organized their own Masses tended to use cheap sliced bread for the eucharist, in a gesture of solidarity with the underprivileged. More upmarket Masses would go in for brown wholemeal or a few tasty croissants. A few feisty Young Turks, eager to get in touch with the masses, clamoured to use hamburger and Coke for the eucharist, but were slapped down by others who insisted that these were unacceptable not because they were untraditional but because they did not constitute food and drink. Then, in a revolutionary move, the Vatican decreed that wine as well as bread could now be used for the eucharist. There were teething troubles with this visionary new dispensation. One elderly priest at Westminster Cathedral, shaking with nerves at his first Mass with wine for the people, grotesquely overdid the supply and filled several large chalices with the stuff. It proved, however, to be a sparse congregation that morning, and since each of them took only a shy sip of the unfamiliar liquid, the priest found himself bearing six and three-quarter chalices of consecrated wine back to the altar after communion. Since this was now the blood of Christ, he could not of course pour it down the sink or lay it aside for a booze-up later. Instead, he began dutifully quaffing it off, chalice by chalice, until he was clutching on to the altar to keep himself upright. After the ceremony a group of altar servers carried him off into the sacristy and deposited him in a chair, where he could sleep his eucharist off.

The *éminence grise* lurking behind the more political currents of this resurgence was a Dominican friar named Laurence Bright. It was several years after we had become friends that I learnt that his name was actually Ronald, and that Laurence was his religious name. This came as a mild version of the jolt one might experience in discovering that one's wife was a professional assassin, or that one's aunt was really one's mother. He was a tall, willowy man, part cherub, part satyr, with an improbably large, grey-thatched head, huge, *faux-naïf*, absurdly erotic blue eyes, flaring clown-like nostrils and a pouting sensuous mouth. He cooed rather than spoke, and his body was so long, knobbly and rubbery that he seemed to have permanent trouble in keeping its various stray bits and pieces reasonably united. He was a connoisseur of small absurdities, and would pounce on them with the delighted yelp of a botanist discovering a rare species of plant. He had something of a camp, suavely malicious manner, though its origin – if the two could be distinguished in those days – was less queerness than the quadrangle, and he would lounge sardonically down a snow-bound street wearing only a shabby clerical suit and his trademark, surreally long blue scarf. The suit was too short in the sleeves, so that there was a touch of an overgrown Dickensian orphan about him. He looked like a cross between an Edwardian roué and Dr Who, and how he had washed up as a friar seemed only slightly less of an enigma than cosmic wormholes or the Bermuda triangle.

He had, in fact, started out as a card-carrying agnostic. He had been a nuclear physicist at Oxford, and at the time was evidently well to the right of the Tory Party. But at some point he became an Anglican, perhaps, so some speculated, in reaction to some of the military uses of his scientific work. He was, in effect, working on the atomic bomb. Then, somehow, he drifted from high-Tory Anglicanism into the Catholic Church and left-wing politics. This was perhaps partly because of his relentless intellectual clear-sightedness: once he had persuaded himself that capitalism was morally disreputable, he put his unsavoury past behind him with characteristic briskness and never looked back. But there was also, despite his air of a spiritual *flâneur*, a strain of going the whole hog about him, which might help to explain some of these otherwise eccentric shifts of allegiance. Roman Catholicism was a kind of logical step from Anglicanism, and getting himself ordained rather than just cheering from the back pews was another such pushing of the matter to its inexorable limit.

Something of the same aversion to the middle ground maybe accounted for his curious trek from far right to far left, though this had its logic too. In a sense, he transferred his Wildean disdain for the suburban masses from élitist contempt to revolutionary politics, as indeed did Wilde himself. Being a radical socialist simply supplied Laurence with a whole new set of reasons to find the middle classes irresistibly amusing. Patrician *hauteur* could thus be converted into radical courage. I have seen this over the years with a number of public-school Marxists, who are brought up to be afraid of nobody and can then place this enviable insouciance at the service of the political left. It is the ex-working-class radical who wonders whether he ought to wear a tie to the left-wing book launch. Perhaps Laurence was conscious of his incongruity, as a bizarre blend of Brideshead and Bolivia, Evelyn Waugh's Anthony Blanche and a guerrilla fighter. He knew, no doubt, that his incessant cooing, camping and satiric chortling would have been grotesquely out of place in a trade union meeting, but the qualities these things reflected also meant that he wouldn't have minded. Anyway, the British Communist Party at the time, with whom we Catholic leftists had a brief, uneasy association, was stiff with types who would have been filed by Central Casting for walk-on parts as country squires, scout-masters or classicist dons. In fact quite a few of them *were* scout-masters and classicist dons.

Laurence may have been an oddball on the left, but he was nonetheless granted the accolade of the other man who influenced me most at the time, Raymond Williams. Williams met him briefly, and commented to me later that he was 'a real man'. Since Williams was reluctant to concede reality to most of the people he encountered in Cambridge, this was a genuine compliment. Like myself, Williams felt ill-at-ease with the flamboyant semiotics of English upper-class life. Indeed, the fact that he did depressed me, since I hoped that by the time I reached his age I might have outgrown the impulse to smash in the face anyone who brayed rather than spoke in restaurants, sported a cravat or said 'rarely' when they meant 'really', and Williams was ominous evidence that I might not. But he was shrewd enough to see through Laurence's Mertonian mincings to the unswerving commitment beneath. He could see that he belonged with the class of foppish secret agent who fusses over his brand of mustard but could kill you with a matchbox. Certainly Laurence could give people a nasty knee-jerk in the ideology while seeming only to pass the time of day, from which it would take them weeks to recover.

Anyway, Williams himself knew all about the crossing of class signals. He was a source of perpetual faint bemusement to his Cambridge colleagues, since though he clearly had a world-class mind he also wore his hair at collar-length, rolled his 'r's' like a Cornishman, wore roll-neck sweaters and looked more like a farmer than a don. He had the wrong voice for his placidly authoritative air, and the wrong face for his superbly unruffled poise. His very presence deranged the conventional categories, and his fellow dons gathered inquisitively round him like zoologists around a dolphin whose low droning might just be a recitation of the *Iliad*.

Despite his mildly raffish air, Laurence lived a threadbare, hand-to-mouth sort of existence. He had no real function within the Dominican order, but this meant that he could live the on-the-hoof life of a friar to the full. As a cross between Oscar Wilde and a footloose cleric, he made himself up as he went along, sauntering from pray-in to anti-war demo in a scintillating piece of self-improvisation. His upper-class grit allowed him to live without anchorage or nostalgia. Though he seemed extraordinarily self-sufficient, he must surely have been lonely, but he remained suitably stiff-lipped about it. Like a lot of clerics, he compensated for the loss of his traditional comforts by being a highly skilled scrounger, who could relieve you of the price of an upmarket meal as fast as he could say eschatology; but Catholics understand that their clergy need to be consoled for their fleshly deprivations, and are not averse to tipping them a few bob. When I travelled on a bus as a child with my father, and a brace of priests or clutch of nuns clambered on board, my father would always pay their fare for them, and signal shyly to them that he was doing so, though they were almost certainly a good deal better off than he was.

Laurence, to be sure, was somewhat selective in his fleshly deprivations, ending up in a covert relationship with a young woman who had come to him to take instruction in the Catholic faith. I knew of several examples of this kind of spiritual backfiring at the time. It was a bit like consulting a psychiatrist for alcoholism and finding yourself having a glorious piss-up with him. Another priest who found himself in this situation, a former scientist like Laurence, told me with grave irony that since he and his client had been discussing the Church's teaching on sexual morality, he regarded their subsequent sexual congress as 'practicals'. It reminded me of the time when I was about to get married to a Catholic, and was told by the local curate that since I had been brought up in the Church, I 'wouldn't need all twelve lessons, just the six'. The idea that one could have lessons in being married seemed strange, and I wondered what they might consist in. Surely not trial sex in the sacristy? Cookery, perhaps?

It turned out to be instruction in the theology of marriage, though I had scant faith in the theological credentials of the curate. On my first visit to him, I passed a young man, evidently under similar instruction, walking away from the priest's room with a bemused, faintly desperate expression on his face, while the curate stood at his door bellowing after him in a broad Northern accent: 'Don't worry, it's all a mystery! It's all a mystery!' These words were the standard formula for explaining away any patent absurdities or illogicalities in Catholic doctrine. If you couldn't quite bring yourself to believe that God wore a tartan jockstrap, you could console yourself with the reflection that how or why he did so was all a mystery. I had once heard this same curate give a sermon on the ascension of Jesus into heaven, which began with the words: 'There are a lot of things we'd like to know about Our Lord's ascension, such as how did he manage it?' It was not quite the high theological tone of a Laurence Bright.

It was at Laurence's suggestion that a group of us, mostly Catholic undergraduates at Cambridge, launched a left-wing Catholic journal called *Slant*, which ran throughout most of the 60s and caused something of a fluttering in the cloisters. The name of the journal, indeed the very same design, was finally adopted by a porno magazine, which Laurence spotted one day in a Soho shop-window and gleefully circulated to the former editors. Nowadays people write the odd doctoral thesis on the Catholic left, which I suppose is one up from oblivion. But it was Laurence Bright who finally liberated me from my stiff-necked papist correctness. I was a socialist, to be sure, but I was anxious to know how far to the left a Catholic could go without falling off the edge. So I asked

Laurence, who replied with a coo and a cavalier gesture, 'Oh, as left as you like.' It seemed there was no edge after all. The New Testament's answer to David Lodge's question 'How far can you go?' is, of course, never far enough. And only a Catholic would think it was about sex.

Laurence died of stomach cancer while still fairly young. He died in his brave, brisk, thoroughly commonsensical way. Not long before his death he visited me in Oxford with his partner, an accomplished organist. I watched him standing by himself in the college chapel as she played one of his favourite organ pieces for him, head bowed, shoulders hunched, still in his tattered clerical suit despite his errancy, looking as usual like an elongated question-mark. He knew he was dying, though I did not. He shall always stand like that, listening with head bowed, in my mind.

2

Catholics

The boy who first revealed to me the facts of life was clearly a Protestant, since he seemed to have read a little scripture. As the hair-raising news of human reproduction assaulted my scandalized ears, I resorted to the only defence available to me. 'Well,' I rounded on him, 'maybe that's how *Protestants* do it . . .'

Just as the convent bore only a tenuous relation to reality, so did Catholicism as a whole. Its esoteric doctrines seemed no more applicable to everyday life than trigonometry was applicable to pressing your trousers. Like magic, it was a highly determinate system but entirely self-confirming, with all the exceptional clarity of an hallucination. Catholicism was less about good deeds than about how to keep the charcoal in your thurible alight or knock another fifty years off your allotted time in purgatory. It was less about charity than candelabras. We were pious and heartless, strict-minded and mean, pure-living and pagan. There was a crazed precision about the Church's doctrinal system, rather like those geography textbooks which record the height of Mount Everest as exactly 29,006 feet, or railway timetables in some ramshackle region of the world which announce the departure of a train at 11.03 a.m. It resembled the insane exactitude of the psychotic whose mathematical calculations are impeccable, but who is carrying them out perched on a window-ledge thirty floors up. For some, this might sound a reasonable description of literary theory.

All this bred a peculiar kind of intellectual neurosis, such as wondering whether the Pope's declaration of his own infallibility was itself infallible. Like most Catholic children, I made my first confession at the age of seven, which the Church judged in its pre-Freudian way to be the age of reason. But I was worried about how far back I had to go in recalling my sins, since I was not certain exactly when, scientifically speaking, my seventh birthday could be said to have begun, or whether an act committed on the very dot of becoming a rational entity could be sinful. It was a Beckettian universe, at once rigorous and absurd. Everything was both definitive and elusive, in a strange blending of mystery and transparency.

In that sense, perhaps, it was the usual world of childhood writ large, since childhood is a mixture of self-evident truths with an alarming inability to grasp what is going on. Like Beckett, too, it was a world of compulsive rituals, not of agonized inwardness. In soundly anti-Cartesian spirit, you did the proper thing and the appropriate state of mind would follow. As with the acting technique of Laurence Olivier, you built from the outside inwards, and so were at odds with a social order which made a fetish of interiority. You kept your charcoal alight and your incense dry and trusted that the rest would thereby be given unto you.

You were raised, then, to be suspicious of the warm glow, the intuitive certainty, the ineffable private experience. Truth had to be publicly argued for, reasoning was to be respected, and the criteria for inner states lay in what you did. You could baptize a baby dying in the womb by inserting a water-filled syringe into its mother's vagina, since what mattered was the action itself, not human relationships or contexts of meaning. The magical and the materialist were thus closely allied. One Easter Sunday, a Catholic priest of my acquaintance encountered on the street his Anglican opposite number, who raised his hand in greeting and called out to him joyously: 'Christ is arisen.' The priest's comment in private later was unequivocal: '*Silly bugger.*' Religion was not something to get all sloppy and personal about; it was more like launching a ship than falling in love, a set of public rites to be precisely executed. Unlike the Anglican clergy, you did not clasp someone's hand in both of yours on first meeting and stare meaningfully into their eyes.

A Catholic aversion to subjectivism went along with a working-class allergy to emotional ostentation, and both were underpinned by an Irish devotion to the tribe rather than the individual. Going to confession was about as emotionally stirring as buying a pound of carrots. It was certainly not confessional in any sense that Oprah Winfrey would recognize. A radical stress on material practice, on the public, collective, symbolic dimensions of selfhood, was entwined with a callous impersonality which could make even Stalinism seem sentimental. The Church set its face against all phoney subjectivism, and was as indifferent to individual feelings as a psychopath. One of the few attempts to humanize religion I recall was the priest who tried to argue us out of impure thoughts by reminding us that 'the Blessed Virgin has breasts too'. This was about as effective a remedy for adolescent lust as urging a drunk to bear in mind the tawny sheen of a glass of Glenfiddich.

Catholicism was a world which combined rigorous thought with sensuous symbolism, the analytic with the aesthetic, so it was probably no accident that I was later to become a literary theorist. You did not see reason and mystery as incompatible. There was no danger that you could murder God, or a poem, by dissection. If the universalism of your faith encouraged you to ride roughshod over the particular, all those garish icons recalled you to what could be seen and handled, to the material world as signifier or sacrament. Yet it was a deeply un-English culture even so. To be Catholic was not really to be English, rather as being a Jew was not. They were both alternative cultures, as opposed to being, say, a Congregationalist, which hardly seemed a culture at all.

But though you were a minority yourself, you were not brought up to prize the crankish or lovably idiosyncratic, to rejoice in the thought that there's nowt so queer as folk, or clamorously approve of him who stands alone. You were rather more English in not particularly admiring innovation, since what millions of men and women had found fit to believe over the centuries seemed a surer guide to the truth than the fancy notions some eccentric loner had dreamt up overnight. But you were not an English liberal in relishing plurality as a virtue in itself, or thinking that it would be a funny world if everybody thought the same. On the contrary, you considered that it would be a splendid world if everybody thought the same. You knew that it took all kinds to make a world, but regarded this as a misfortune rather than a virtue.

This is not, perhaps, as Neanderthal an attitude as it seems.

If cultural diversity is part of what makes life worth living, it has also brought a great many lives to a bloody conclusion. The call to celebrate such diversity is nowadays the merest cliché in the mouths of theorists and politicians; but it is only when cultural difference can be taken for granted, rather than defiantly affirmed, that it will have ceased to be a source of conflict. It is also likely that far fewer people would have been slaughtered and abused if all human beings had been black, gay and female from the word go, apart from a few males and heterosexuals here and there to keep the species ticking over. To affirm human difference without reckoning the terrifying price we have had to pay for it is the kind of liberal sentimentalism which Catholics, for all their aberrations, were trained to sniff out.

You grew up as a Catholic, then, lacking all instinctive feel for the liberal sensibility. If this was a grievous loss, it also allowed you to see what was wrong with it. Conversations were not strewn with nervous qualifiers or mined with self-doubting disclaimers. There was no particular virtue in not being certain. You did not doubt your faith for a moment, not because you were magnificently steadfast but because it was not the kind of thing that could be doubted, any more than one might query the existence of pubic hair or prime numbers. Faith is a cleaving to whatever you find you cannot walk away from, however hard you try. What we find ourselves unable to relinquish even at the point of death, when it is ourselves that we relinquish, is definitive of who we are; and this is not on the whole something we can choose, like a hat or a hairstyle. But you cannot have faith in what cannot logically be denied. You could not doubt your personal commitment to God because you had no personal commitment to him, any more than you had a personal commitment to the Panama Canal or the concept of near-sightedness. You did not value something because you had chosen it, but chose it because you thought it valuable. Later, as a student at Cambridge, I was to flirt briefly with existentialism, but this was just a high-falutin way of announcing that I was a depressed, disoriented late adolescent, as post-structuralism was to be for some of a later generation.

One can move fairly freely, then, from Catholicism to Marxism without having to pass through liberalism. The path from the Tridentine creed to Trotskyism is shorter than it seems. My own school involuntarily produced a distinguished socialist barrister, a full-time organizer of the International Marxist Group, the most left-wing member of the executive of the National Union of Teachers, a clutch of radical philosophers and economists, and myself. Friends who discover today that we all attended the same school imagine that it must have been the kind of place where doped-up pupils swing barefoot from trees all day, vote to abolish physics lessons, couple openly on the lawn and call their teachers Jane and Sam. But it was simply an obscure Catholic grammar school which was unwittingly transmitting a sense of cultural alienation to its students, along with some of the conceptual tools by which they might make sense of it.

Despite the benighted autocracy of their church, Catholics are prime candidates for the political left. They are, at least in Britain, usually of working-class immigrant stock, are taught to value systematic thought, feel at ease with the collective, symbolic dimensions of human existence, and are wary of subjectivism. They also understand that human life is inherently institutional, prize communal tradition over individual inspiration, and believe that things are alarmingly bleak but could be unimaginably better. Like socialists, they are far too down-beat for progressive-liberal taste, and far too hopeful as well. They also inherit a fertile tradition of ethical and political thought, and are not afraid to think ambitiously. As the most enduring cultural institution which history has ever witnessed, surviving across the farthest-flung pockets of space and time, Catholics know a good deal about historical change, but a lot about continuity as well. In all these ways, few types could be less easily recruitable to the ranks of postmodernism. Being expected to believe in papal infallibility and the Assumption of the Blessed Virgin, not to speak of learning to excuse torture and moral brutality, being sexually assaulted by priests or battered by sadistic nuns, was admittedly a high price to pay for this schooling, but one had to take the kicks with the ha'pence.

But Catholics also tend to the left because of their instinctive aversion to liberalism, which is both admirable and disabling. They make good authoritarians, a species which socialism has attracted in plenty. It is one of the left's embarrassments that its eminently reasonable project exerts an irresistible fascination for those who need to work out their father-complexes or resolve their Kleinian ambivalence. Any socialism which fails to base itself upon the great liberal inheritance, for which Marx had such profuse praise, is likely to prove bankrupt. So Catholics and leftists need to learn from liberals about the mixed, ambiguous nature of things, the charm of nuance and singularity, the difficulty of determinate judgements, the preciousness of the fleeting and fragile, the pathological shyness of truth. Liberals, for their part, need to learn that when it comes to the major political conflicts which rive our world, there is no standing judiciously in the middle. In each of these cases someone is roughly in the right of it and someone else in the wrong of it; and in clinging to this faith, non-liberals are in the right of it.

We Catholics were of course a minority in England; but we did not value the marginal or minoritarian, in the manner of a later postmodernism. On the contrary, it was we who had a monopoly of truth, and the majority who were out of line. They were the deviants from our orthodoxy, the bulging periphery to our slim centre. While we rested calmly upon metaphysical certitudes, they blundered around in the outer darkness spouting such absurdities as religious tolerance and the notion that Jesus might not have been an only child. Like many a minority group, we combined arrogance with paranoia, the self-satisfaction of the elect with the malicious anxiety of the insecure. We also combined the dissidence of the outsider with a conservative will to belong. It was rather like being a homosexual Tory or an *haut-bourgeois* black. Or, indeed, like being an Ulster Unionist. The Queen was never as much ours as she was the Protestants', and there was always a hollow croak in our patriotic cheering, a mild sense of duplicity.

My North-of-England grammar school was almost wholly populated by Irish teachers and clerics, along with second-generation Irish pupils. But I was unaware that names like Doyle or Farrell or O'Dwyer were in any sense out of the ordinary, since I have no memory of the words 'Irish' or 'Ireland' being used throughout the whole of my school career. Naturally not: the task of these raw-boned, huge-handed Brothers, themselves refugees from small farms in

Clare or Kerry, was to wipe the last traces of bog from our souls and pack us off into middle-class England. It was not wise in these circumstances to tout an intimate knowledge of hurling, or betray the fact that one returned home in the evening to parents with Waterford accents. We were Irish, but we did not know we were, even if most of us came from families embarrassingly larger than the English sociological norm.

The school launched us out into bourgeois Britain with enviable success. It had an especially distinguished geography master who infiltrated a bit of geology into us on the side, and one day he was busy informing us that a particular piece of rock was so many millions of years old. A small boy at the back of the classroom, with a rural Lancashire accent so thick that he sounded like an Albanian hot-foot from his very first English lesson, put up his hand and asked: 'Please sir, 'ow do we know?' Gratified that he had sparked a rare flash of intellectual interest, the master explained a little about carbon dating. The boy in question, now based in the USA, is one of the world's leading vulcanologists, and when I once happened to fly near an active volcano in the States, I could be sure that he was perched in one of the small scientific aircraft which were darkening the sky around us. Now, no doubt, he knows all about how we know.

The headmaster of the school, Brother Damian, was a white-haired career sadist from an undistinguished Irish town called Ballyjamesduff, whose only other achievement had been to produce Henry James's grandfather. Helping to nurture one of the world's great novelists, however, was hardly sufficient compensation on the town's part for bringing forth Brother Damian. He ought certainly to have been strangled at birth, or buried alive in infancy in some desolate stretch of bogland. He had the solid physique and florid complexion of an Irish farmer, but was to exert his muscular energy on maiming small boys rather than digging potatoes. Another Irish-peasant Brother, with a passing resemblance to a psychotic turkey, taught woodwork, and rumour had it that the floorboards of the woodwork room concealed a number of fresh young corpses, their flesh carved by chisels into occult designs familiar to Freemasons or Knights Templar.

Damian spent his life in charge of the spiritual development of children, and had about as much human understanding as a tortoise. Though he did not actually lower the trousers of his teaching staff and beat them strenuously on the bottom, he treated them in every other way as he treated the first-formers, so that teachers and pupils were thrown together in an unspoken pact of loathing and dread. It was a point of pride with him to discourage sinful individualism by not knowing a single one of his pupils by name. Since several thousand pupils must have passed through his hands, most of them literally so, this was an achievement on a level with discovering a new galaxy or biological species. He was as indifferent to individuals as a lavatory attendant, and regarded his students simply as potential sources of academic glory. Anxious to inculate English ways into his Gaelic flock, he made us play rugby, sing the national anthem, and meticulously recorded our fathers' occupations. I remember my father's sudden choked silence as, sitting to obedient attention before this moral monstrosity in his study, he was asked abruptly what he did for a living, and responded in an unnaturally loud voice with the only lie I ever heard pass his lips.

It was a morally bankrupt, superbly successful school, packing off the odd pupil to Cambridge, as high-risk a business then as a moon-shot in the early days of rocket science, and generally grooming the gifted sons of Eirin for English stardom. Brother Damian finally retired to a religious community in Dublin, where he enlivened his last days by terrorizing young novices. I read his obituary in some journal or other, and noted how it avoided acknowledging what a contemptible bastard he was by concentrating coyly on his cleanliness. In the end, all the world could find to say of the boy from Ballyjamesduff was how spotless his clerical collar was. I heard later that his brethren in the Dublin community had refused to gather around his deathbed to pray for his soul, as stunning a rebuff as if the royal family were to renounce horse-racing. Perhaps his fellow-clergy sensibly concluded that there was no point in praying for any such clearly mythical entity as his soul. In death as in life, he represented much of the truth of the Roman Catholic Church.

I grew up, then, amidst secrecy and doubleness, absolute refusal, Gothic grotesquerie, gestures of extremity, ginger-tufted virgins, rituals of asceticism and self-immolation, death-in-life. No doubt all this helped to shape my politics later, if only because it was as far from the world of middle-class Protestant England as the mountains of Afghanistan. But there is much to be said for suburban rationality, and a good deal of peril in such living near the edge. It is a modernist lie that extremity is estimable in itself, just as it is a conservative myth that normality should *ipso facto* be cherished. Socialism and Christianity are at once ordinary and otherworldly creeds, valuing the common life but seeking to transfigure it. For Christian faith, the love of God is a subversive, uncompromising force which breaks violently into the world, rips apart families, pitches the mighty from their thrones, raises up the lowly and sends the rich empty away. It is by such revolutionary irony or reversal that the Yahweh of the Old Testament identifies himself.

At the same time, no creed could be less extremist and more mundane. For Christianity, one is saved not by some exotic cult or ritual, but by the quality of one's ordinary, unglamorous relationships with others, by feeding the hungry and protecting the widows and orphans from the violence of the rich. It is of this that Yahweh has to keep irritably reminding his tiresomely cultic people, who seize any opportunity they can to scamper off and fashion a few idols. As Charles Taylor has suggested, the affirmation of ordinary life finds its origin in Judaeo-Christian spirituality.* Perhaps the two ideas – of the life of the spirit as an extreme affair, and as something humble and unremarkable – come together in the quaint Messianic doctrine that when the Messiah comes, he will transform the world out of recognition by making minor adjustments.

In the end, I refused co-optation, but only just. I shopped around religious vocations exhibitions, draughty halls in which every religious order in the country set out its stall and tried to drum up recruits. There was the only order with identical-twin priests, life-size effigies of Africans being shown the light, the waist-nipped *haute couture* habits of nuns you felt you could pick up and tinkle like tiny black

---

* See Charles Taylor, *Sources of the Self* (Cambridge, 1989), Part 3.

bells, the rattle of Carthusian rosary beads as big as meatballs and the incessant braying of Dublin brogues trying to bellow you into a lifetime of serving up spaghetti for some crew of self-flagellants on the Mile End Road. Then, before I knew it, one smooth-talking, productivity-conscious vocations director, who handed out pictures of the Sacred Heart as furtively as if he was doling out pornography, had dropped the shilling in my glass and whisked me off on a trial-offer, sale-or-return trip to a seminary near Oxford, mildly astonished to find that the seminarians said 'bloody' and played guitars.

My arrival at the seminary was not auspicious. I was only thirteen, on my first rail trip alone, and made such a neurotic mess of the journey that I arrived hours late, just after midnight. The place, a rambling Victorian house of several storeys, was in darkness, and it was beginning to snow lightly. I rang the ornate iron bell on the front door, and after what seemed ten minutes or so saw a light go on at the very top of the house. After a while the light went off again, and another light came on in the window directly below. This downward alternation of light and darkness was repeated, and I took it that someone was descending a staircase. There was another lengthy interval before I heard a fumbling with chains and bolts and the door swung open. An irascible-looking prior, with an comically large head like a reveller in a Mardi Gras carnival, stood on the threshold, dressed in dowdy puce pyjamas with a heavy black clerical cape slung hastily over them.

I explained who I was and stammered out an apology, but he turned dismissively on his heel and disappeared into the darkness of the hall. I assumed that I was meant to follow him, and trotted along behind him clutching my bag. I was used to dealing with cantankerous clerics. He led me at a cripplingly brisk pace along an ill-lit corridor until we arrived at a carved wooden door. This, I imagined, might conceal a staircase leading to my room, but a faint, familiar waft of musty incense drifted out of the door as he creaked it open, and I realized that this was the chapel. To my surprise, the prior asked me abruptly if I would care to say a prayer before retiring. Perhaps this was meant as some kind of penalty for arriving late, or perhaps it was the custom of the house. Praying was the last thing I felt like doing, but I was in no position to refuse. It would have been like being invited out to dinner and refusing to eat. He reached behind the chapel door, switched on the light, offered me a curt goodnight and stalked off down the corridor.

I sank down in the nearest pew and tried to rid my mind of the image of the prior's mutely furious descent of the stairs. The chapel light was flickering wildly, casting shadows over the grotesque statues lining the walls, and after a minute or so it sputtered out altogether, leaving me in total darkness. I rose to my feet, groping my way blindly from pew to pew until I reached the door. The door swung open easily, but as I closed it behind me something cold and moist smote me softly on the cheekbone. It was a snowflake. I had come through a door which led to the outside of the house, and had just heard it lock behind me. The front door, with its ornate iron bell, was waiting for me a few yards away.

I was fascinated during my brief stay in the seminary by Brother Kenelm, an elderly lay brother so mild, white-haired and beatific that he looked as though he had been sent to the place from Central Casting. For a good two decades he had done nothing but lay out the spoons at mealtimes, which he did with all the scrupulous precision of a nurse in an operating theatre. He would while away an hour or so each morning shambling up and down the long tables in the refectory, crooning a hymn to himself as he laid down spoon after spoon in its appointed place. No spoon had ever been found less than perfectly perpendicular to the edge of the table, or either a millimetre nearer to or further from its neighbouring knife than any of its colleagues. From time to time, Kenelm was gently encouraged to extend his sphere of activities to encompass the knives and forks as well, but when this suggestion was put to him he would respond with a serenely non-comprehending gaze, like an aborigine eyeing an anthropologist.

Quite unwittingly, he was to teach me more about the inner meaning of the clerical life than anyone else. I had noticed that despite his pathological indolence he was especially eager to help female visitors on and off with their coats, an activity which allowed him to fondle their breasts. He got away with this by the flagrancy rather than furtiveness with which he did it, so that those who observed this doddering old soul brazenly pumping a woman's chest would simply refuse to believe their eyes. Traditional Catholics refused to believe it because they assumed that, being a cleric, he must be holy, while more sophisticated Catholics refused to believe it because they assumed that, being a cleric, he must be gay. Indeed, he and I were almost the only heterosexual members of the community, though he was a good deal more conscious of the fact than I was. As far as the rest of our brethren went, the answer to how one separated the men from the boys was, as the old joke has it, with a crowbar.

Some of the priests were generous-hearted alcoholics, or, as one might say, plastered saints.

Despite his godly, geriatric appearance, Kenelm was astonishingly successful with women. It was as though his appearance was a kind of front, just like his trousers. Like several of the seminarians, Kenelm's solution to the question of whether or not to wear trousers under his habit was to wear trouser-bottoms only, which were fastened by elastic below the knee. These were known jocosely in the community as 'flasher's trousers', since they were said to be favoured by sexual exhibitionists who wore them with a raincoat and nothing else. But I once came across him strutting through the centre of town in a gaudy Hawaiian shirt and tight white jeans, with a young woman on his arm. Like the Carmelite convent, he was two worlds stitched cunningly into one, and it was impossible to spot the join.

I had assumed previously that what sexual impulses I had would vanish on ordination, like acne or a fondness for rhubarb pudding, that one might grow out of libido as one does out of nappy rash. The difference between the young and the old is that the young still believe in the concept of maturity. But the Church had taught me prudence, and though I had no particular objection to celibacy at the age of thirteen, it seemed the kind of thing I might one day develop, like stubble or schizophrenia. I was also warned off the religious life by a dejected-looking lay brother whom I came across in the seminary kitchens one afternoon, emptying gigantic cans of beans into a surreally large cooking vat and stirring them glumly with an outsize wooden spoon, like a giant in a fairy tale. 'You're not going to do it, are yer?' he asked me in an alarmed, incredulous tone, as though I had announced my intention of leaping from the roof or inserting my finger into the bacon slicer. Not long afterwards I returned home to my crestfallen parents, a spoilt priest.

3

Thinkers

Imagine a visitor from outer space who lacked the concept of combining different sorts of goods. On his planet, some people go in for the long jump, while others collect jade statuettes and yet others design rococo gardens, but no one dreams of doing all these things together. Arriving in our own culture, this visitor begins by imagining that he will have to choose between such goods just as he does back home, until he discovers that there is one particular good on earth which allows you to move between all these other goods with a minimum of effort. It is a kind of meta-good or magical distillation of all others, and its name is money.

Not long after this discovery, the alien would no doubt come to grasp two other facts about money, which sit somewhat awkwardly together. One is that the pursuit of it engages almost everybody's energies almost all the time, while the other is that it is held in hearty contempt. The alien would be instructed by high-minded stockbrokers that you can't take the stuff with you, and informed by corporation executives that the best things in life are free. Psychoanalysts would tell him that money was a superior form of shit, while maudlin characters propping up the bar at his elbow would insist that the moon belongs to everyone. Money would soon come to seem to the visitor a metaphysical conundrum, at once nothing and everything, impotent and all-capable, meretricious bits of metal which men and women will nonetheless kill to accumulate.

One explanation for this paradox is that though money is not everything, it is an indispensable condition of almost everything. It is not true, for example, that love or sunsets are free of charge, since you cannot have a decent relationship or an aesthetic experience if you are starving. Persons are by no means priceless, as insurance companies are well aware. Money is the capacity of capacities, so protean and commutable as to bring with it the promise of untold diversity. It is the narrow vestibule, itself meagre and unremarkable, which gives you access to a dizzying array of opulent chambers. If it is at the root of almost everything, it is because it *is* potentially almost everything. The fact that we value money not for itself but for what it brings is one reason why even the most venal among us can declare truthfully, with hand on heart, that money is not so important. There are indeed a great many more things in life than money, and it is money that gives us access to most of them.

There was not much of this metaphysical conundrum in 1950s Salford. The boys at my primary school were sometimes so famished that they shovelled great mounds of beetroot into themselves at lunch, then spewed it up again in steaming maroon heaps on their school desks. A lot of them would have known alcoholism and grotesque physical violence at home, and were dripping with all kinds of dark, horrifying sexual knowledge. I was a puny, livid-faced Oliver Twist among these scabby-kneed roughs, dispensed from being regularly bullied only because I was chronically ill. I also happened to share a desk with the cock of the class, the boy who could thrash all the others, and lived under his patronage and protection. The boys seemed in a permanent state of frantic aggression, their lives as much governed by rococo rituals as a Trappist monk's. There was no rationalist non-sense about needing a reason to fight, any more than you needed a reason to break wind. The lads were driven by ferocious tribal loyalties, had the sense of honour and blood-obligation of a Palermo pimp, and a range of experience as limited and repetitive as a fruitbat's.

Some of them seemed as immune to physical pain as a stove-pipe. They could endure any amount of punching and caning, not least at the hands of a teacher known as Miss Arseole, whose real name I can now retrospectively recon-struct as Miss Horsehall. You could have crushed their tes-ticles in a vice and they would not have whimpered, but they howled inconsolably if they ripped their shirts in a fight, since this meant confronting the wrath of parents who had no money to replace their clothes. I was the only child who wore a coat to school, on account of my delicate health, which marked me out as sinisterly as if I had arrived at school in a Bentley with a caviar lunch tucked under my elbow. The coat made me a target for violence as surely as flaunting some obscenely taunting slogan on my chest, though it also signalled that I was a kind of moral cripple, and so inhibited the aggression it provoked. It was like a wolf offering his throat to a rival in the course of a fight. There was no cloakroom in the school, since there were no coats apart from my own. The playground lavatory was a stinking, festering affair that a Bombay beggar would have thought twice before using. Even if you did use it, there was nowhere in the school to wash your hands afterwards. Hygiene was as alien to us as Heidegger. For holidays some of the boys went off to what was known as the bread-and-jam camp, since that was the only food they got there, and to warm their beds in winter they used a brick heated in the oven. We were one of the few families to have a bath, though it was too rusty to use.

It was the kind of school where most of the pupils probably never encountered more than three trees at a time until they were well into their twenties. Even then, we had the conviction that once you had seen one tree or flower you'd seen the lot. Most of my relatives found real flowers something of a come-down after artificial ones. There was not much Nature in the city. There was a river, but not even canned fish could survive in it. News of Nature, of a world not fashioned of blackened brick, filtered through to us from time to time, but it seemed as remote as Sussex or Jupiter. It was hard to say what Nature was for. Even if it had jumped into our laps we would not have known what to do with it. On the whole it seemed a bit of a waste. You could spend ages waiting for it to do something. Not that my own family would have wasted time staring at it, any more than we would have sat for hours staring at the plumbing.

These days I believe fervently in Nature, though not in any Wordsworthian sense. Even though I still find it hard to tell one tree from another, and despite my affection for Oscar Wilde, I am convinced that the postmodernists are wrong to be so deeply in love with the constructed, the invented, the self-fashioning. Piously opposed to universal truths, they generalize what it feels like to live in Manhattan to the entire globe. On the contrary, what governs our lives for the most part is the given, the habitual, the sheer inertia of history, circumstance, inheritance. It was a Saul Bellow character who remarked that history was a nightmare during which he was trying to get some sleep. The apparently radical belief in perpetual change, mobility, plasticity, is a fantasy largely in the service of the status quo. It is capitalism which arrogantly imagines that everything is possible, and socialism which acknowledges in its more modest, materialist way the heavy ballast of legacy and circumstance. Most Americans seem to be reared on the hubristic belief that you can crack it if you try; the United States is a society ridden with tragedy yet with scant tolerance for failure. Materialists, by contrast, are aware of how narrow our margin for manoeuvre really is. If change were just down to the will, it might never come about at all. The will, after all, is as much an historical product as whatever it struggles to transform. It is because change, too, has a smack of necessity about it that it can occur. Even the urge to freedom is a kind of fatality, as the former rulers of empires have long since conceded.

Literacy was not the strongest point of my childhood community. It was a world which would no more have understood how you could make a living by writing books than how you could make one by picking wax from your ears. My Irish grandfather on my mother's side once stumbled across a pair of glasses in the street, put them on and wore them for the rest of his life. But he did not have a lot of use for them, since his eyesight was fairly sound and in any case he could not read. They just seemed an imaginative addition to his face. He would ask me as a child to read aloud to him details of various stocks and shares from the newspaper. He did not understand this occult information any more than I did, but I think he harboured some private fantasy that he was a stockbroker. I once asked him when he left school, to which he replied cunningly: 'A quarter to four.' At about the age of nine or ten I became gripped by the conviction that I should read the classics, though I had no idea what the classics were, whether they were one or several books, books by one or many authors or whatever. My mother, who had no more notion of what the classics were than I did, took me to a second-hand bookshop in the middle of Manchester, where I browsed embarrassedly around for a while and came across an old set of the complete works of Dickens. I think it was on sale for five pounds, but the bookseller allowed my mother to put down a deposit of two shillings and sixpence and pay off the rest weekly. I still have the books on my shelf.

I read the books in between fits of asthma, bouts of delirium, and prayers offered up for the release of whichever godforsaken soul in purgatory was furthest from the door. In a sort of supernatural division of labour, we were taught to pray to an exotic variety of saints, though later on, being a natural-born rebel, I refused to deal with sub-committees and went straight to the Management. I enjoyed the Dickens novels without really understanding them, unaware that I was in the process of becoming that most archetypal of post-war characters, as much part of modern mythology as the Mad Scientist or the Dumb Blonde, the Scholarship Boy. I was devouring *Dombey and Son* while some of my classmates were still struggling with *Pip Is A Dog*.

But I could already dimly sense that this hot-house preciousness was as much a disability as an advantage. It was obscurely linked to my sickness, and both illness and the intellect sequester you from the common life. When I was told that I had passed the examination for the local grammar school, I was already well-schooled in the event's momentous implications. I knew that if the outcome had been different I might have spent the rest of my life in industrial working-class Salford, with no time between factory shifts to finish off *Bleak House*. Some years later, as a second-year student at Cambridge, I came back to Salford to work in a local soap factory during the summer vacation, and ran into some of my old schoolmates who had full-time jobs there. We eyed each other, surly with embarrassment, across the gaping social abyss. They were lifers; I was passing through *en route* to higher things. The factory made a soap called Imperial Leather, and some of my workmates thought 'Leather' was a posh way of pronouncing 'lather'.

But though Salford is the subject of a book entitled *The Classic Slum*, it could also boast a distinguished cultural heritage. In the 1930s, it was home to an agit-prop group called Red Megaphones, which won itself an enviable reputation throughout the European working-class movement. It became home in the same period to the great Communist folk-singer Ewan McColl, who was deeply involved in the city's socialist militancy. Through McColl, Joan Littlewood of Theatre Workshop, pioneer of cultural experiment in the East End of London, took a keen interest in the place, and was later to advise a young playwright from the neighbour-hood near my school, Shelagh Delaney of *A Taste of Honey*, to set up a popular theatre in the town.

My mother remembers young Walter Greenwood, author

of the wildly successful novel *Love on the Dole*, swanning around in his new-found finery, *en route* to the Big Smoke. As a young girl, she also saw L. S. Lowry painting by the roadside. There was a bookmaker's called Finney's, and Mr Finney's son Albert won himself a scholarship from the local grammar school to the Royal Academy of Dramatic Art, a singular phenomenon in those days. It is unlikely that his father would have placed a bet on it. But it helped that working-class accents were just coming into fashion, and Albert was to make his name as the truculent young prole in the film *Saturday Night and Sunday Morning*. I saw him return to the area to play Luther in John Osborne's play, witnessed by his proud relatives. Lowry, Delaney, Finney: the Irish émigré influence was evident. Salford is also the home of the composer Peter Maxwell Davies and the film-maker Mike Leigh.

Not that the place was bereft of philistines. The story is told of a meeting of the city council which was trying to agree on a way of brightening up the town, a task which in my view would have required little short of divine intervention. Eventually, one councillor proposed erecting a few pagodas in the local park. The suggestion met with general approval, until the mayor rose heavily from his seat. 'It's all very well having these 'ere pagodas in t'park,' he growled, 'but what I want to know is this. *Who's going to feed the buggers?*' It was the same mayor who, while conducting a visiting dignitary around the city art gallery, proudly assured him that all the works on exhibition were 'hand-painted'.

Later in life, I was to overcompensate for the uncertain literacy of my early environment. Whereas other academics worry about not being productive enough, my embarrassment has always been the opposite. Instead of finding myself unable to write books, I find myself unable to stop, to the point where some people have wondered whether I am actually a committee. Indeed, in the salad days of English academia, when publishing books was regarded as slightly ill-bred, I was denied one or two jobs because of this vice. While colleagues struggle to placate their publishers, assuring them that the manuscript will be delivered in eighteen months' time, I have to conceal from my publishers the fact that I completed it a good two years ago.

It is, of course, a disgracefully privileged problem to be plagued with, and like incest or zoophilia one almost impossible to discuss with anyone else. Colleagues with whom I try to air my disability look sick and haggard and turn on their heel, as though I was grousing about having too much money or being ravishingly handsome. Perhaps there is somewhere in the world an Authors Anonymous, where the over-productive can gather discreetly in small supportive groups, able to declare without shame that they have just binged on a theoretical treatise or knocked off four essays in a row. One would begin, no doubt, by acknowledging that one was powerless to switch off the computer, and that refraining from reviewing for more than a few days required the aid of a force greater than oneself. In time, one might learn to slim down to a paragraph or two a day, or ring a fellow sufferer for help when one felt a three-decker novel coming on. In the meanwhile, however, when every other disabled group has its fund-raising, public relations and political lobby, we overproducers are still the pariahs or unacceptable ones, feeling the resentful silence which falls over the company as we stroll self-consciously into the room, trying pathetically to pass ourselves off as normal, psychically blocked, unproductive academics.

I write as much as I do largely because I enjoy it, as people might enjoy frottage or chicken livers, and I have never quite got over the scandal of being paid to do what one finds gratifying. My father, who worked for thirty years in an engineering factory which never yielded him a single pleasant moment, thought the idea of enjoying your job the most sublimely utopian one imaginable. He could conceive of nothing more paradisal. One day someone will no doubt blow the whistle on us literary academics, let the cat out of the bag, and draw some bureaucrat's attention to the fact that we actually are paid for reading poems and novels, as someone might be paid for sunbathing or self-abuse. The shameful truth will then be exposed to a jeering, incredulous world, that as a result of some extraordinary administrative error we have been treated for a century or so on much the same level as those who research into cancer or post-colonial poverty.

Intellectuals who stem from the working class may sometimes relish this sort of work more than those who regard it as part of their birthright, but this need not mean that they always rate it all that highly. Indeed, there are reasons peculiar to their background why they may not. Those from the social margin are less likely to be rationalists or idealists, inflating the role of ideas. What, one might ask, have ideas ever done for them? This is especially true of women, whose material conditions make them on the whole less spontaneously idealist than men. It is generally men, not women, who tug you by the elbow when you are trying to weave your way through the traffic on Fifth Avenue and ask you your views on phenomenology. But it is perhaps true also of those scholars who spring from less well-heeled circumstances. One must be deeply invested in the idea of rationality, acting as a custodian of reason in a world of lethally irrational forces. *Ratio* is a question of proportion, and proportion is a question of justice. Yet there is a madness of reason too, and reason is not what is most fundamental to human life, which is not to say that what is fundamental to it is un-reason. It is easier to describe this double-think than to live with it.

Much of the philosophy that matters is therefore also anti-philosophy. Anti-philosophers are those who find philosophy problematic for philosophically fascinating reasons, not just those who are indifferent to it like Cher or Brad Pitt. In a similar way, anti-autobiography means not just not writing your autobiography, an astonishingly prevalent practice, but writing it in such a way as to outwit the prurience and immodesty of the genre by frustrating your own desire for self-display and the reader's desire to enter your inner life. Even inside some quite conventional philosophers there is an anti-philosopher struggling to get out. 'To make light of philosophy is to be a true philosopher,' wrote Blaise Pascal, and as the man who gave the world the first syringe, wrist-watch, calculating machine and public bus service, not to speak of establishing the theory of the vacuum, his words ring with a certain authority. Socrates, the father of philosophy, was something of a clown, ironist and self-proclaimed ignoramus. There cannot be professional philosophers unless there are also cooks and stonemasons. Only on the back of an economic surplus can you float a full-time intelligentsia; before that point, the thinkers have to pitch in with the hunters. 'I think, therefore somebody has been doing the donkeywork' might be the anti-Cartesian motto of this vein of inquiry. The German philosopher Fichte developed a theory which he named Transcendental Egoism; but as someone once observed, one would like to know what Mrs Fichte thought about that. 'He thinks, therefore she does the dirty work' would not be a bad catch-cry for feminism. Or perhaps: 'He thinks, therefore she is not allowed to.'

Some of the most creative intellectuals have been those who have affirmed and debunked the life of reason in a single gesture. Seamus Heaney once remarked that while poetry engaged his entire being at one level, he felt pretty indifferent to it at another. In that reservation, one can hear his Derry small-farmer background speaking. What if others win for you by their sacrifice the very largeness of mind which might tempt you to betray them? Is this not a tainted gift? Is it bread or a stone?

On the other hand, I have known working-class intellectuals who took ideas far too seriously. I once published a book dedicated to my two older children, and was surprised to read a review of the work which was devoted largely to attacking the dedication. I had heard of reviewers who never got past a book's Introduction, but not to have struggled your way past the dedication seemed to mark new heights of literary endeavour. The book was a self-declared Marxist study, and the reviewer, a recovered Stalinist, objected to what he saw as my children's middle-class names, which seemed to him inconsistent with the work's political drift. Perhaps, he observed pleasantly, I should have named my children Sid and Albert. I happened at the time to be teaching a working-class Londoner from Ruskin College in Oxford, a pugnacious little Cockney who drew me conspiratorially aside and asked me what I intended to do about the review. What was there to do? I asked with a shrug. 'Nah', he replied impatiently, 'I mean what yer gonna do about '*im*?' I gave him the same reply. 'Look', he said, 'you just say the word and I'll tell the lads, OK? I mean, they don't need to know who this fucking geezer is, right? You just say the word, mate.'

Fergus was another working-class intellectual of my acquaintance. He was a waiter at one of the Cambridge colleges when I was a young Research Fellow at another, and we first met in the pub where Fergus spent most of his off-duty time. He was a burly, rather alarming-looking Glaswegian with a nose so grossly inflamed that it had become something of a Cambridge institution, along with tea at Grantchester and punting on the Backs. His nose was not in fact just inflamed but a kind of intricate system of nodules, pits and crevices, of sudden shifts of plane and tiltings of perspective like a Cubist painting, impossible for the eye to take in as a single unified phenomenon. With its complex sub-systems of bumps and multilayered nostrils, it seemed to defeat any simple three-dimensional logic, like some purely imaginary form known only to mythologers or mathematicians. Teams of cartographers working night and day might just have mapped its flushed, crumpled folds. Slopes of flesh which one expected to drop smoothly in a natural incline towards the nostrils would suddenly have second thoughts and turn upwards again, before levelling out into a cratered, rubicund surface. Hair seemed to sprout not only from his nostrils but from every pore of his entire nasal apparatus, almost thick enough to warrant a daily combing. Just as there is no natural limit to knowledge, so there was in principle no end to exploring Fergus's nose, which viewed in various lights and from different angles would disclose arresting new features hardly visible before.

Fergus and I had drunk together for years without either of us really knowing who the other was or what he did. Then I was invited to lunch at another college, and when a puffed, trembling hand holding a cheese board suddenly thrust itself between myself and my host, I could sense in a dim flicker of recognition that Fergus was on the other end of it. We gazed at each other in mute, embarrassed surprise, like brothers bumping into each other in a brothel. Once Fergus knew that I knew what he did, he felt constrained to convince me that he was more than a simple college staff member, which I had no trouble in believing. Working at a rather eminent college, he had dished out the cheese to a fair few media moguls and cabinet ministers, and had the number of most of them. One celebrated author had chatted away one evening at High Table in his pukka English accent, amusing the company with a joke which involved a rather poor imitation of a Scotsman. Only the silently observing Fergus, who had known this man as a fellow urchin in Glasgow, realized that this was a Scotsman imitating an Englishman imitating a Scotsman. He was thus not without connections in high places, and once, when the Pope was about to visit Britain, drew me confidentially aside to let me know that he was thinking of bringing His Holiness into the pub should he happen to set foot in his college. It struck me that this would be an unlikely occurrence, but that if anyone could get the Pope into a pub it was Fergus.

He had an unstaunchable flow of persuasive talk, in which the line between fact and fantasy was not so hopelessly blurred that one could not discern the odd chunk of truth from time to time. He probably had, as he claimed, drunk with Brendan Behan while he was living in Dublin, and told me the story of how Behan was once working as a housepainter while also scribbling the odd spot of journalism for the *Irish Times*. Finding himself painting the *Irish Times* building, he would occasionally nip off his ladder through the window, type out some thoughts for the newspaper, then scramble back on to the ladder again. Fergus was likewise a working man with cultural aspirations, who penned the odd poem and had wrestled with Joyce in his time. He had a fine tenor voice too, if a touch stentorian, and could crack your vertebrae with the higher notes of his pub renderings of 'The Yellow Rose of Texas'. Walls heaved and buckled, bloodhounds dived whimpering for cover, peasants in the Mekong delta raised their faces puzzledly to the sky, and the hair rose in unison, as if in salute, on the backs of fifty goosepimpled necks.

I shall always regret the evening I almost killed him. Fergus's college had decided to take action on his nose, which the Fellows considered was becoming something of an embarrassment at High Table. Some Cambridge conservationists took a contrary view, arguing that the nose was a precious feature of the local landscape and should fall under the protection of the National Trust. But the reformers won out, and the college paid for him to enter a clinic for an operation. I went to visit him there bearing a bottle of whisky, only to learn as I handed it over that his operation was not, as I had imagined, already over but only a few hours off. Since he was therefore not allowed alcohol, but was certain to take a few swigs from the bottle once my back was turned,

it seemed possible that I had just stumbled upon the definitive solution to the nose problem by dispatching him to
eternity. He slung the bottle casually under the bedclothes,
and I was relieved to hear a faint clink; obviously he had a
whole bar stashed away under there. At least, then, as with a
firing squad with one rifle loaded with blanks, it would be
impossible to tell which of his numerous bottle-bearing
visitors had actually done for him.

Ludwig Wittgenstein was a classic anti-philosopher, a philosopher of astonishing genius who had little time for the
discipline, advising his disciples to give it up and do something useful like medicine instead. As a child he had built a
sewing-machine entirely out of matchsticks, and made it
work. He was fascinated by anything that slotted, whirred,
cranked, articulated, not least language. Perhaps this sceptical stance to the life of ideas is part of what I find attractive
in him, though I could no more build a sewing-machine
than could a wombat. He was also for a while an aeronautical
engineer in Manchester, a city in which my father was a
rather less grand kind of engineering worker. To become
what he was, Wittgenstein had to beat a retreat from fabulous
Habsburg wealth, whereas I had to turn my back on the
opposite condition.

Of all the anti-philosophers, then, Wittgenstein is the one
who has pursued me in various incarnations throughout my
life. He cropped up first when I was an undergraduate at
Cambridge, as my supervisor there, Dr Leo Greenway, had
been a minor member of his intellectual circle. The only
recorded reference to my supervisor by the great man is a
sentence which begins: 'If we were to take Greenway here

and boil his head . . .', which I can imagine Greenway, who always had a crush on mighty minds, regarding as an egregious honour. And indeed, one would rather have one's head boiled by Wittgenstein than one's back slapped by Heidegger. Many years later, when the two men had drifted apart, Greenway spied Wittgenstein from the window of his college room, looking frail and ghastly. He was, in fact, dying of prostate cancer. Greenway, struck by the Austrian's corpse-like appearance, considered running out to greet him, but then thought better of it. He never saw him again. In this as in most other respects, Greenway was impeccably English.

Wittgenstein next showed up as a political influence, when I was involved in the Catholic left movement of the 1960s. This was the Wittgenstein of the *Philosophical Investigations*, who sought to root meaning in forms of practical life and the public use of signs, to overthrow the fetish of interiority. The *Investigations* reads like an assemblage of images or snatches of narrative, wonders aloud with Socratic *faux naïveté*, asks us questions which may or may not be on the level. The feints and ruses of the book's language proceed by aphorism, dialogue and homely exemplifying, distilling a whole complex argument in some peasant-like dictum or casual epiphany. There is the sense of a mind in playful, ironic dialogue with itself, deceptively lucid in expression but teasingly enigmatic in content.

It is the idiom of a man effortlessly at home in the world, which was the very last thing Wittgenstein was. Like the Freudian analyst, we suspect that the author has a few answers to hand but is keeping them up his sleeve, forcing us into the labour of self-demystification, persuading us by his hospitable style to lower our guard so that he can run the odd ring around us. For him, the truth is concealed only because it lies so palpably on view that we miss what is under our noses, distracted as we are by the snares, *trompe-l'œils* and false bottoms of language. We overlook the scandalously self-evident, preferring to peer astigmatically at the world through our imposing metaphysical spectacles. Philosophy is something of a mug's game, though it takes an emperor to perceive that the emperor is naked. It was in this spirit that Wittgenstein remarked disparagingly of Freud that it took one Viennese to know another.

Frege is a philosopher's philosopher, Sartre the media's idea of an intellectual, and Bertrand Russell every shopkeeper's notion of a sage. But Wittgenstein is the philosopher of poets and composers, playwrights and novelists, and snatches of his mighty *Tractatus* have even been set to music. There is a Dutch cassette on which you can hear lines from the work croaked and warbled in an hilarious stage-German accent. Perhaps the fascination he exerts for artists is partly because of the fabular, mythological quality to his riches-to-rags career, a case of life outdoing art. He was socially disadvantaged, in the sense that he sprang from a ludicrously well-heeled family; and though he struggled hard against this disability, giving most of his money away and proclaiming that it was 'better to go without shoes', he could never quite eradicate its lethal traces. He was certainly a profoundly strange figure, whatever his commitment to common forms, the rough-and-ready stuff of our ordinary speech. So people think I behave eccentrically? he once asked. It is as though they are staring through a window at the curious motions of a man outside. They do not know that there is a storm raging out there, and that the man is keeping his feet only with the utmost difficulty.

Wittgenstein kept his feet with immense labour, and the least gust of dishonesty would have been enough to bowl him over. He was grotesquely ethical, whatever the humble, workaday tolerance of his later philosophy. On first hearing the commonplace English expression 'It takes all kinds to make a world', he caught his breath and observed that it was a most beautiful, kindly saying. But human kinds other than his own were not generally to his taste, and he was well practised in brusquely casting off any friend who crossed him. He was an arresting mixture of monk, mystic and mechanic: a high European intellectual with a yearning for Tolstoyan *simplicitas*, an irascible authoritarian with a thirst for holiness, a conventionalist in philosophy who betrayed all the cavalier disdain for convention of the aristocrat. He lived a secret homosexual life while insisting that everything lay open to view, and as a reactionary remnant of the Austro-Hungarian empire seems to have got on far better with Marxists than with dons.

As a private in the First World War, Wittgenstein puzzled his military headquarters by constantly demanding to be transferred to more dangerous postings in the field. The nearness of death, he hoped, might shed some light on his radically unfulfilled existence. But he was not at all afraid: he felt that his life was at some level beyond harm, hidden away, unassailable, which is perhaps the deepest keynote of comedy. With the drafts of the *Tractatus* in his pocket, he crouched on the extreme limit of language with the darkness of death at his back, and was struck dumb. You had to demarcate what philosophy could legitimately say, all those not terribly important things, from those vital matters about which it had better remain silent, and to which Dostoevsky and detective thrillers, Tolstoy and bad American movies, St John and Mendelssohn might yield the odd clue.

The early Wittgenstein is homesick for the pure ice of philosophical precision, for those countless gleaming metaphysical acres stretching silently to the horizon. It is a beautiful vision, but he came to see that if you tried to walk there you would fall flat on your face. To walk, we needed friction; so the later Wittgenstein abandons the crystalline purity of his exacting youth and seeks to return us to the rough ground of our mixed, ambiguous, everyday speech. But nothing could be more at odds with the pluralistic, demotic, open-ended inquiries of this later work than the man himself: autocratic, haughtily patrician, driven by a fatiguing zeal for moral perfection and afflicted by that strange mania known as Protestantism, for which everything is a potential sign of salvation or damnation. If only he had learned to be a little less moral, he might have been more assured of salvation. As it was, he was marooned between the ice and the rough ground, at home in neither.

And so, detesting Cambridge, he kept running away, usually to extreme edges: a hut on a far-flung Norwegian fiord, a monastery garden in Austria, a rough stone cottage on the west coast of Ireland. He even took flight to the Soviet Union in the darkest days of Stalinism, turned down a chair of philosophy there and asked instead to be trained as a medical doctor. His enthusiasm for the Soviet Union was more Franciscan than Leninist: it was the cult of labour which attracted him, and no doubt the autocracy as well. I, too, detested Cambridge, if small things may be compared with great, and ran away in the end, but I only made it as far as Oxford. It was rather like taking refuge from insincerity in Hollywood. Wittgenstein escaped from Cambridge to Ireland, while I was later to escape there from Oxford.

Indeed, it was in his Irish incarnation that I encountered him next, when I took part in the unveiling of a plaque at his cottage in Killary harbour in Connemara. I had written a novel about Wittgenstein in Ireland, *Saints and Scholars*, and was later to write some of the screenplay of Derek Jarman's film *Wittgenstein*, in which hunky young men in black leather jackets, for whom Spinoza is probably some kind of pasta, shamble around thinly disguised as philosophers. Local legend has it that when Wittgenstein lived in Ireland's sublimely beautiful Killary harbour he tamed the birds, though he also seems to have irritated some of the residents with his demands that the dogs stop barking. He made only an imperfect St Francis.

For the unveiling of the plaque, an act performed by one of the few national Presidents who was both female and had actually read some Wittgenstein, the cottage was crammed cheek-by-jowl with Irish philosophers and Irish-speaking local fishermen, and some of the locals had less than genial memories of their imperious foreign visitor. It was here that he wrote much of the *Investigations*, some early drafts of which a local man called Tom Mulkerrins, who fetched him his turf, was ordered to burn in a tiny outhouse. God knows what mind-buckling human insights were immolated on the west coast of Ireland in 1948. I had met Tom Mulkerrins some years before, when I arrived in Ross Roe, the tiny fishing harbour where Wittgenstein had taken shelter from the storm, and asked him whether he recalled a foreign scholar who had descended on them many years ago. Something in his manner made me hesitate. 'I'm not the first to ask you this, am I?' I said. 'Neither the first nor the forty-first,' he replied impassively. Perhaps they could have set up a local Wittgenstein industry, with T-shirts emblazoned with 'The World Is Whatever Is The Case' intertwined with a couple of leprechauns. I showed Tom Mulkerrins a reference to himself in Norman Malcolm's memoir of Wittgenstein, which did not impress him in the least.

Wittgenstein was at school with Adolf Hitler, while another anti-philosopher, Bertolt Brecht, was fifth on the Nazis' blacklist. Next to Brecht's typewriter, in true anti-philosophical style, stood a small wooden donkey, with a sign around his neck which read: 'Even I must understand it.' Perhaps such creatures should be compulsory issue for cultural theorists. Brecht believed that thinking ought to be 'a real sensuous pleasure', even if he challenged the Romantic dogma that our thought is artificial but our feelings natural. He knew that feeling is a matter of custom, imitation, theatre. Though he was a German, he tried as hard as he could not to sound like one, penning a spare, muscular, aphoristic prose very far from Hegel's. When he brought the Berliner Ensemble to London, he told them to act his plays like greased lightning, just to confound English prejudices about bovine Teutons. He was an uncompromising avant-gardist, who remarked that putting a factory on stage would tell you nothing about the nature of capitalism. Oddly for an avant-gardist, however, he rarely wrote about his own barbarous age, and produced drama which ordinary men and women could appreciate. He was said to look like a cross between a Jesuit priest and a long-distance lorry driver, and he always had exactly three days' growth of beard, a remarkable biological phenomenon. He was that amphibious animal, a middle-class plebeian; his real name was Eugen, but he thought Bert sounded less cissy.

Brecht was a Marxist, but a Marxist maverick, who in a rare badge of honour was banned from the Danish Communist Party before he even applied to join. He never went anywhere without a packed suitcase, changed countries oftener than his shoes, and in consciously anti-heroic fashion kept his head well beneath the parapet. He lied his way past the McCarthy Committee on UnAmerican Activities (the FBI's file on him stretched to 1,000 pages), and on settling in the German Democratic Republic after the Second World War practised what he once called 'Chinese exile', a crafty mixture of outward conformity and inner dissent. He referred privately to Stalin as 'Honoured Murderer of the people', but this did not stop him running a Stalinist theatrical showcase, or denouncing the East German workers' uprising of 1953.

Brecht was a true theatrical revolutionary – 'We're not playing for the scum who want the cockles of their hearts warmed,' he once snarled to his actors – whose ideal theatre was a cross between a circus, a laboratory and a boxing ring. If the theatre could become a kind of sports arena, ordinary people might come into their own as shrewdly appraising specialists, alert but not solemn, relaxed but analytical, 'thinking above the action' as he liked to say. Nothing refutes the myth of the mindless masses more unarguably than their sporting expertise. The actors, for their part, must find some way of signalling what they are not doing in what they are.

They must indicate that there is always more production where that came from, and make their behaviour look impermanent so as to demonstrate that history is like that too. In the famous alienation effect, they must 'quote' their parts rather than become them; empathy was a tool of fascism, not socialism. Indeed, Brecht had a soft spot for amateur actors because of the unwitting alienation effects which their bungling performances kept throwing up. For all this to work, you had to break the audience's infantile desire for suspense. If Brecht had directed *Waiting for Godot*, he would have hung a large sign at the back of the stage reading 'He's not going to come, you know.'

All this Brecht could have placed in the service of some struggling theatre group in the GDR, allowing them to trade on his internationally celebrated name. But he preferred his establishment theatre, which guaranteed an unbroken flow of fine cigars, just as he put women boldly at the centre of his dramas while shamelessly exploiting them in real life. He had the machismo of the classical male revolutionary, but it was also a toughness he would come to need. He could see nothing in tragedy but a bourgeois cop-out. His idea of tragedy was wholly conservative, a matter of implacable destiny, unalterable human nature and fearful submissiveness; it was just that whereas the conservatives celebrated this model of tragedy, he rejected it. Otherwise, he and they were wholly at one on the subject. Like most avant-gardists, he had a touch of virile triumphalism about him. Curiously, he seemed to believe that the mere fact of historical change, whatever its actual content, was somehow comic. In one of his fables, Herr Keuner returns to his village after a long absence to be cheerfully informed by his neighbours that he hasn't changed a bit. 'Herr Keuner,' Brecht writes, 'turned white.' In his eagerness to advocate social change, he could not admit that some forms of loss are absolute, and this in the age of Buchenwald. The camps proved perishable, but not for those who perished there. He did not see that the denial of tragedy is as much a cop-out as the affirmation of it.

My own earliest experience of peddling ideas to the masses, a project which was later to become my full-time occupation, was through a student job as an encyclopedia salesman. I was a grade B salesman, which meant that I did not come into physical contact with the general public – a fortunate constraint, given my shaggy, uncouth appearance at the time. My job was rather to set up home visits for kosher, grade A salesmen by telephone. This I did by being assigned a particular telephone area, working backwards through the telephone directory (in case some rival firm was working forwards), and ringing up everyone in that area at a suggestible time after dinner to inquire whether they were part of the dwindling minority of black-hearted parents who were jeopardizing their children's future by refusing them access to educational books. We were not allowed to use the word 'encyclopedia', which was thought to have fusty, forbidding overtones, or to suggest that anything as sordid as a commercial transaction was involved. This double prohibition made the act of selling an encyclopedia somewhat less straightforward than it might otherwise have been. My instructions were to give my contacts the impression that I represented a non-profit-making educational trust with a scientific interest in the intellectual development of the child.

The telephone area which I had been assigned was classified by the company as a *Britannica* blackspot. This did not mean that its inhabitants actually bought *Britannica* or even considered doing so, just that if they were asked what encyclopedia they might buy in the extraordinarily unlikely event of their ever doing so, *Britannica* was the only answer likely to occur to them. I had never actually seen the books I was selling, or had any assurance that they actually existed, but I could describe their contents fairly exhaustively in the rare event of being called on to do so. Most of the people I rang up, however, either did not understand what I was saying or refused immediately. It was not this which finally forced me to abandon the job, but the emotional strain of dipping in and out of complex human dramas. One middle-aged man I rang mistook me for his blackmailer and broke down sobbing, perhaps taking my inquiry as some subtle refinement of psychological torture. Those waiting for vital phone calls greeted me with accusing coldness, while others would assume funny voices, assuming that I was a friend doing the same. The lonely and desperate would demand the most recherché details of the books simply to relish the sound of another human voice.

Complaints about my invasion of domestic privacy were surprisingly rare, though one householder, whom I pictured as some sort of barrister, interrupted me after one sentence of circumlocutory script to ask testily whether I was trying to sell him an encyclopedia. This was an impossible question for me to answer, containing as it did two censored words, but before I could recover he went on: 'I resent this intrusion into my home; I think the practice is despicable and I wish you would desist.' Then he put the phone down. I admired this off-the-cuff eloquence, and wondered what he was doing in my largely plebeian telephone area. Most of my contacts were too cowed, baffled or inarticulate to pluck such perfectly formed protests out of the air.

Encyclopedias are not of course the only way of popularizing knowledge. There are also the various bluffer's guides to molecular physics, Buddha for beginners, Spinoza made simple and the like. I was once in an Oxford bookshop when I noticed a colleague of mine, a distinguished Oxford philosopher, browsing his way through a volume of *Philosophy Made Simple*. Seizing the chance of a jape, I crept up behind him and murmured: 'That's a bit difficult for the likes of you, isn't it?' He swung round with a start, but to my dismay it was not my colleague at all. It was a complete stranger. I had the vague impression that he was a tourist. Somewhere in the world there is a man who has reason to believe that Oxford is such a snotty place that strangers step up and sneer at you in bookshops when you are furtively trying to better yourself.

Henry was not a philosopher, anti or otherwise. He was a warehouseman at a department store in Manchester, where I worked during the summer before my Cambridge final exams. I spent my lunch hours in the canteen reading Aeschylus and Racine, mugging up for the Tragedy paper, and Henry once encapsulated the difference between us in a pithy observation: 'You know what?' he told me one day. 'You've read more fucking books in the two weeks you've been here than I've read in my fucking life.' He went on to make an exception of what he called 'one-handers'. One-handers were soft porn mags you held in one hand while the other hand was otherwise engaged. Aeschylus was clearly not that.

While not especially deep in Hegel, Henry was given to philosophizing in his own way. He would sometimes voice his opinion that 'we can't be the only ones here', 'here' meaning the universe rather than the department store, and there was a mournful, metaphysical streak in him which unsettled his more pragmatic colleagues in the warehouse. There was something slightly poncey about such expansively cosmic comments. He was not given to horseplay or ribald sexual fantasizing about the female staff, though he did keep in his pocket a faded paragraph cut from a tabloid newspaper which reported on a Corsican fisherman who was said to be the proud possessor of 'thirty-two inches of uncontrollable flesh'. There were fierce debates among the men in the warehouse about whether this meant 'slack' or ' 'ard'. But I felt that Henry's own interest in this monstrous organ was more scientific than prurient, in line with his general curiosity about the cosmos. He was also something of a multi-culturalist, a view strongly contested by most of his workmates, and once told me that he had no objection to any ethnic group, 'Poles, Scotch, Yanks, Indians, Greeks, the lot.' He then reflected for a moment, before adding: 'Barring Italians.' He was a liberal pluralist, but not uncritically so. We had that in common too.

Henry behaved genially towards all of his colleagues except Padraic, a curmudgeonly, thick-legged Cork man with jowls like a bloodhound whom he treated with cutting, tight-lipped contempt. It was only much later that I realized that Padraic was his father. Padraic, whose job was to operate a machine which crunched up cardboard boxes, spent the whole day pulling the same lever over and over again, like some doomed figure from Dante's *Inferno*. But you had the sense that he reaped some perverse satisfaction from this godforsaken task; it was real work, not like the effete floor-cleaning, rubbish-collecting and shelf-stacking that the rest of us nancy boys got up to. We were factotums, while he was an artisan. He was obsequious to the bosses, and you felt that he would gladly have chewed the cardboard himself if the machine had snarled up. Henry and Padraic never exchanged a word and went home separately after work, though it was the same home they went back to. They resembled each other about as much as a koala bear resembles a packet of pork scratchings, and their blood-relationship seemed as much some grotesque accident as being struck by lightning in bed or bitten by a black mamba.

During my second month at the store, Padraic lost his footing while trying to climb into his bedroom window, having lost his house keys during a pub crawl. He fell to the pavement and shattered his skull, killing himself instantly. Henry took the morning off for the funeral, but otherwise turned up to work as usual. He did not comment on his father's death, though to my astonishment he volunteered to take over the infernal cardboard-crunching machine. This might have been out of some sense of filial duty; but I had the impression that what looked like an act of conformity was more an act of rebellion, proclaiming his freedom from his father by demonstrating that he had no need to make a gesture of refusal. Taking over his father's old job was a way of defining him as just anyone, and thus of snuffing him out in the very act of appearing to inherit his mantle.

4

Politicos

Some time in the 1980s, I was banned from joining the Labour Party at a time when other people were leaving it in droves. This was a peculiarly ignominious experience, like fighting tooth and nail to scramble on board the *Titanic*, or finding oneself dressed as a Viking at a party where everyone else is in evening dress. For the Labour Party to keep people out at that time seemed as absurd as Marks & Spencer barricading their doors to keep customers at bay. It was not even as though I *wanted* to join the Labour Party. I had been instructed to do so by a far-left organization of which I was then a member, and which had warrened the local Labour Party from end to end like a revolutionary rabbit. Like most paranoiacs, then, the party officials were quite right to be suspicious. They really were being taken over by aliens. But it sounded such a hackneyed fantasy that whenever they complained about it they were scoffed at as authoritarian bigots.

I was called to interview by the local party's executive committee, an array of stony-faced bureaucrats one or two of whom I vaguely recognized as having served me the odd meat pie or pair of socks over some shop counter. Instead of being asked my views on nursery schools or how best to fight the Tories, the sole intellectual member of the committee asked me courteously whether I was a reformer or a revolutionary. This struck me as a low-target, off-bounds, uncomfortably intimate sort of question, like asking me whether I suffered from haemorrhoids or had ever had sex in the bath; but I responded at considerable length, exhaling a thick fog of obscurantism as I cast elaborate, footnoted doubt on the distinction between reform and revolution while hoping that the assembled company would be unable to follow a word. At this point, a harassed-looking middle-aged woman interrupted me with the chilling words: 'Mr Chairman, I may be a very simple person, but . . .' This one lethal phrase was enough to blow me out of the water. They were not interested in my views on the difference between reform and revolution; they were interested in unmasking me as a bloody intellectual who, even if he was as politically sound as Gordon Brown, talked a lot of nauseating gobbledygook the likes of which had never been heard in the back bar of the Crown and Anchor.

I was then asked whether, if I was admitted to the party, I intended to continue selling the newspaper of my group. I replied that I did, knowing that it would be unconstitutional for them to refuse membership to someone who sold a journal which did not promote non-Labour candidates, as our newspaper did not. But they briskly set aside their own constitution and refused me entry anyway. Things had gone too far for fair play. I returned to my group and told them glumly of my failure, secretly glad that I might now have just one evening a month free of political work. The Labour Party later let me in, long after it was worth joining.

The group to which I belonged had, like most such set-ups,

broken away from an even more puristic one. Such fissiparousness has been second nature to the far left, and poses the intriguing scholastic problem of how few people can be said to constitute a political movement. Just as the scholastics fussed about how many angels could dance on the head of a pin, so the left's inherent tendency to split raises a number of tricky metaphysical questions, akin to the physicist's search for the smallest possible building block of Nature. The main policy of this original group had been one of strenuous non-intervention. In fact the group abstained from political activity with all the scrupulous attention to detail with which other groups picketed and demonstrated, exhausting themselves with their principled inertia. They would chase up and down the ranks of other people's marches, handing out leaflets to explain why they were not taking part in this revisionist, centrist, class-collaborationist venture. Its members would return home and stew mindlessly in the bath, drained by the fatigue of not demonstrating.

It was not always easy to distinguish this group from a *Daily Telegraph* readers' circle, since their chief theoretical case seemed to be a virulent contempt for the working class. Under capitalist influence, the working class had grown warped and arthritic, and though it remained the instrument of world revolution, it was to be trusted no further than you could throw it. The outfit's attitude to the proletariat was rather like that of the Virgin Mary to the baby Jesus, reverently acknowledging his divinity but harbouring no illusions after cleaning up his shit. The question arose as to whether one was allowed to lie to the working class – an academic question, to be sure, since the group had exceedingly few working-class members to be lied to in the first place. Some comrades supported the notion of the 'revolutionary lie', while others insisted that you must tell the proletariat the truth, but, as it were, the 'dialectical' truth.

The truth was not, as the bourgeois ideologists imagined, a matter of facts, states of affairs, statistics, of what was indubitably the case, and other such dismal reifications; it was rather a dynamic, conflictive, constantly evolving affair, so that what was true from one class-viewpoint was false from another, and what was true here and now was not necessarily true 'tendentially', in terms of underlying historical trends. Thus it was 'true', in a static, reified sense of the term, that the whole membership of the organization could have been fitted with ease into a public lavatory (indeed some observers might have considered this the best place to deposit them); but in terms of underlying dynamics the group was many thousands strong. It was 'true', in the boring, trivial sense of the word, that almost all its members were teachers, students, social workers, eccentric upper-class renegades, socially autistic types searching forlornly for human contact, or closet psychopaths eagerly anticipating a spot of revolutionary violence; but dialectically speaking they were doughty dockers and brawny boilermakers to a man. The general idea was that even when they were wrong they were right, a doctrine which a traditional Roman Catholic would have no trouble in grasping.

Dialectics, in fact, was a compulsory topic of study for this organization, and new members had to take lessons in it. Young men and women zealous to smash the bosses found themselves instead sitting stupefied in closed seminars while a senior comrade used a blackboard to demonstrate the mysteries of the dialectic. Instead of learning about exploitation, they were required to take notes on the negation of the negation, or the dialectical transformation of quantity into quality. They had come to create the future and ended up in an algebra class. Quite how the Hegelian unity of opposites was to aid the struggle to keep open a nursery school remained as enigmatic as the Catholic doctrine of limbo, that twilight region where the souls of the unbaptized dwell, which as a child I always confused with a West Indian dance in which the body is lowered to a few inches off the ground. At a socialist conference, I once heard a young worker who had obviously won his spurs in the school of dialectics complacently inform his assembled comrades that 'Kettles boil, dogs' tails wag, and classes struggle.' It was not the kind of stuff which would have escaped unscathed in an Oxford philosophy seminar.

On the other hand, what was wrong with some of the group's philosophical ideas was exactly that nobody in an Oxford seminar would have batted an eyelid at them. The founding principle of materalism, so it gravely instructed its members, was that there was a real world out there, of which we could have knowledge. They did not seem aware that only the odd raving Idealist hiding out in a cave somewhere in Montana would have denied this. Instead, they sported this banal belief as a badge of pride, as though everyone around them, from the village butcher to the First Secretary to the Treasury, entertained some esoteric Buddhist fantasy about the unreality of material things. It was rather like imagining that only you and a few select mates had noticed the remarkable fact that it grew dark every night, and formed a secret club of which adherence to this truth formed the first item of the constitution.

Most of the group's energies were directed not to the conflict with world capitalism, but to the rather more urgent war against other left-wing organizations. For the revolution to come about, it was first necessary to smash the petty-bourgeois illusions of those who believed in strikes, picket lines, anti-nuclear demos, mass protests, the defence of jobs, pay levels, working conditions, hospitals and nursery schools, and other such reformist distractions from the historical matter in hand. In elegantly dialectical fashion, all attempts to build socialism were in fact efforts to undermine it, so that the single most productive revolutionary act was to stay at home and listen to *The Archers*.

The group reserved its high dialectical disdain most of all for those fellow revolutionaries who clung to the 'labourist betrayal' theory of why we were in such a mess. This was the claim that, politically speaking, the working class were chomping at the bit and rearing to go, but were being held back from storming Clarence House and Thames Television by the squalid betrayals of their Stalinist, reformist or 'fake leftist' leaders. Since the group held that the working class, while being philosophically speaking the solution to the riddle of History, were empirically speaking a disreputable bunch of scroungers and layabouts who could do with a smart kick in the pants and a stiff spell of National Service, it indignantly rejected this more charitable theory of their apparent lack of revolutionary ardour.

Neither theory of chronic working-class apathy was actually necessary, since there is in fact no such animal. It is true that there is a scarcity of animated debates over the Asiatic Mode of Production in Halifax pubs, and most people these days are about as likely to turn to Theosophy as to Marxism for a solution to their woes. Enthusiasts for the doctrine of base and superstructure are far outnumbered by devotees of alien abduction. Crop circles are more in vogue than communism, and Rambo is no longer a radical French poet. But there are plenty of heated political debates among working men and women in the pubs and streets in the north of the island I live in. Too many, some might claim. When politics intersects with everyday life, as it does for both good and ill in Northern Ireland, then grocers and fishermen will discuss it even more intensely than football. Indeed, a group of fishermen I know in Northern Ireland keep trying valiantly to stop discussing politics, as you might try to stop drinking Drambuie or taking sugar in your tea, but find themselves simply unable to give it up. The fact that this is not a problem in Cumbria or Canterbury is a comment on the politics, not the people. Try driving a motorway through somebody's back garden or forcing their children to be taught entirely through the medium of Icelandic, and they are likely to become political activists overnight. Those who organize to keep out refugees, or demand the right to defend their private property with cruise missiles, may be reprehensible, but they are not apathetic. Would that they were more so.

It is rational to resist major political change as long as a system is still able to afford you some gratification, however meagre, and as long as the alternatives to it remain perilous and obscure. Such change is discomforting, may prove violent and traumatic, may leave us even worse off in the end, and demands a great deal of us with no certain return on our moral and material investments. Radical politics is thus a thankless business. But it is also rational to resist an oppressive power if one may do so without too extravagant a risk and with a reasonable chance of success. Indeed, it would be astonishing if reasonable men and women failed to do so, as long as they judged that they almost certainly had more to gain than to lose in the process. Once a political system fails to provide enough gratifications to bind its citizenry even grudgingly to its rule, and once reasonably low-risk, realistic alternatives emerge, then one would need a great deal of persuasion to stick with what one knows. Change then becomes as predictable as the word 'like' in the speech of a Penn State freshman. This was as true of the downfall of eastern Europe as it was of the fall of apartheid. We live in a revolutionary age, and radical politics is not at all a thankless business.

My own personal proposal for furthering the cause of socialism would be to abolish sport. Few more crafty ways of deflecting the populace from political action have been dreamt up. If capitalism destroys human community and solidarity, it provides some powerful substitutes for them on the soccer field. If it eradicates history and tradition, it restores them in the mighty annals of sporting achievement. A society bereft of symbolism can brandish its emblems at Wembley or Old Trafford, or even dress up in them in carnivalesque style. Sport is where ordinary people can feel a corporate existence denied to them elsewhere, as well as practising a remarkable expertise to make up for other sorts of deprivation. Like politics, it has its pantheon of legendary heroes, and combines macho drives with aesthetic subtleties. If it releases boisterous energies, it also demands an intricate attentiveness. Since its heroes are glamorous versions of the commonplace, mythical figures yet regular guys, the fantasy world they embody is all the more compelling. Like religion, the truly devout regard sport as a way of life rather than just a weekly ritual. For all these reasons, the instant abolition of sport, with the possible exception of the more tedious sort of board game, should be high on the list of every radical agenda.

Radical politics may not be a thankless affair, but it is an exceedingly modest proposal. Bertolt Brecht once remarked that it was capitalism, not communism, which was radical, and his colleague Walter Benjamin added wisely that revolution was not a runaway train but the application of the emergency brake. It is capitalism which is out of control, and socialism which seeks to restrain it. It is capitalism, as Marx recognized, which is revolutionary to its roots, one extravagant thrust of Faustian desire, and socialism which recalls us to our humble roots as labouring, socializing, materially limited creatures. The postmodern fashion for perpetual reinvention is thus the least radical of attitudes, however it may see itself.

It is a sign of just how bad things are that even the modest proposal that everyone on the planet gets fresh water and enough to eat is fighting talk. One can imagine launching revolutions in the name of some exorbitant utopian ideal, but to disrupt people's lives in such a spectacular way simply so that everyone may be guaranteed a supply of fresh vegetables seems oddly bathetic. Only extremists could argue against it, just as only extremists could endorse a global capitalist system which in 1992 is said to have paid Michael Jordan more for advertising Nike shoes than it paid to the entire south-east Asian industry which produced them. Revolutionaries are those realist, moderate types who recognize that to put such things to rights would require a thoroughgoing transformation. Anyone who imagines otherwise is an idle utopianist, though they are more commonly known as liberals and pragmatists. A student of mine once rather piously informed me that she 'wasn't a revolutionary'. Rather than starting with Hegel, I thought simply of asking her whether she had been reading the newspapers.

Revolutionaries, then, are neither optimists nor pessimists, but realists. Indeed, one reason why they are so thin on the ground is because realism is so extraordinarily difficult a creed to practise. It is exactly this that the street-wise pragmatists fail to appreciate. To see the situation as it really is is the basis of all effective moral or political action, but nothing could be more elusive or exacting. Since the truth, politically speaking, is usually thoroughly unpleasant, being a realist means living a vigilant, cold-eyed, soberly disenchanted sort of existence, perpetually on the *qui vive* for the mildest flicker of fantasy or sentimentalism. Since this is both the only way to live and no way to live at all, radical politics is bound to be a contradictory affair. Its more successful practitioners are likely to be the last people to embody the values of the society they are fighting for – one which would make ample room for fantasy and sentiment – just as nobody would join a club which was tasteless and desperate enough to recruit people like themselves. As a Brecht poem comments: 'Oh we who tried to prepare the ground for friendship Could not ourselves be friendly.'

Realism, however, is in rather more scanty supply in some leftist quarters than a rather crude strain of triumphalism. I recently attended a socialist conference in London at which one young worker rose to proclaim that there had never been so many revolutionary opportunities as at present.

Perhaps he had been sitting for some time in a darkened room with a paper bag over his head, but he was duly cheered and applauded, as that kind of solemnly ludicrous statement generally is in certain left circles. There are those on the left who would still be eagerly expecting the imminent outbreak of revolution while they were crawling through a nuclear wasteland with at least one leg hanging off. In such surroundings, realism is denounced as pessimism, just as it was by the Victorian middle classes. There is a prudish fear of the seamier, more tragic dimensions of history worthy of an end-of-pier comedian. To talk about 'a constant surge forward' and 'the coming emergent mass movement' becomes the merest clichés, rather like more orthodox politicians speaking of how we are living through a time of rapid change, of the consequent need to face severe challenges but also to seize fresh opportunities, of how contemptibly easy it would be for them to win some cheap popularity by actually putting their party's policies into practice, and of how the greatest degree of unity is entirely compatible with the richest amount of diversity.

There is, then, still a clutch of left-wing apocalypticists who predict the imminent arrival of socialism, just as in the USA you can find Evangelical groups who are seriously addressing the question of which TV camera placements around the globe would best record the Second Coming of Christ. But it is, of course, less easy these days for the left as a whole to believe that they have History in their pocket. And this brings with it certain benefits. Just as eras of left insurgency yield one insights which might otherwise be obscured, so the same is true of periods of defeat. Walter Benjamin once plaintively remarked that his prose style would have been less opaque had there been a German revolution, by which he may have meant among other things that to be swept up in a history in the making concentrates the mind even more wonderfully than being hanged.

But it also breeds its correlative vices of purism, arrogance, overhastiness, tunnel vision, a condition in which, since you are on the political up, you can afford to cast off the ideologically impure and look a gift horse brazenly in the mouth. The defeated are wiser than that, if also more prone to jadedness and melancholia. They are also more wryly alert to the limits of the political, which any effective politics has to be. It is the tenderfoot who makes a fetish of the political, and the old-timer who knows there are times when what is needed is less a vote than a double vodka or a blast of Beethoven's Ninth. But it is always possible to fetishize failure too, not least for a radical politics which is all about maintaining a pact with the defeated. How can such a pact come to power without ironic self-betrayal? Yet it is only the liberal who disdains power as such, partly because he has enough of it under his belt, partly because he fails in his privileged way to recognize that power can be emancipatory as well as oppressive. The dispossessed are less likely to underestimate the benefits of power, though only when the very meaning of power has been transfigured out of recognition could they be said to have scored a definitive victory.

The group to which I belonged had broken away from the more sectarian one, and though it retained some traces of this purism it was in general a far less priggish outfit. It is true that, simply to be heard and understood by one's comrades, one had to use certain quaintly formulaic expressions. Events were not planned but 'built towards', and the verb 'struggle' had to be inserted into one's discourse at regular intervals. You did not form a consensus, an opinion or a bus queue but struggled to build towards it, so that 'life's a struggle' was elevated from the status of high cliché to something approximating a philosophical vision. The ruling class did not just perpetrate iniquities, it did so 'over and over again', while comrades did not express opinions about the weather but 'took up positions' on the question, or at least 'struggled' to do so. One comrade, who worked in a local bookshop where he had led a fight for higher wages, told me that this rather genteel agitation by a few elderly, semi-academic bookshop assistants 'had some of the major features of the Permanent Revolution as described by Trotsky'. No doubt this would have come as something of a surprise to the manager of the ancient history section.

Even so, these were shrewd, seasoned, dedicated men and women who fought to protect vital services and could pool a rich fund of experience in order to do so. It is easy enough to scoff at how seriously such minuscule bodies tend to take themselves. Some fifty or so men and women square up to the transnationals and the world militia, earnestly plotting their overthrow. There is a good deal of unreality in this, like Oxford dons who throw themselves under trains because the Bodleian Library has temporarily closed down its stacks; but it is also an instance of the moral principle that in certain situations, you simply have to do the right thing whatever the consequences. Since this is an exceedingly rare principle in political life, it should be cherished for its novelty value alone. You must picket the sweatshop even though you haven't the faintest chance of closing it down, call for the overthrow of apartheid in your editorial even though you know that only 200 people will ever read it. Consequences are important, but they are not everything: one would not refrain from tending an injured earthquake victim just because one knew that in ten minutes' time the building would cave in on him altogether.

Nor did the group have a particular problem with intellectuals in their midst. On the contrary, I found myself attending educational sessions on the Paris Commune, the Bolshevik revolution and the labour theory of value run by young workers who had efficiently mugged up their stuff. The class system was thus gratifyingly inverted. By way of return, I drew upon the full fruits of my professional training by putting the semi-colons into a manuscript which one of the group, a shop steward at the Oxford car plant, had written about his experiences there, and which was later published. While other comrades were specialists in syndicalism, I was a specialist in syntax. I had worked alongside shop stewards once before, when a group of Cambridge academics led by Raymond Williams formed a left forum in the town, which brought together shop stewards from local workplaces who had never met each other before, let alone pooled their experience.

It is generally middle-class intellectuals who have a problem about patronizing the working class and worry about their posh accents; working people themselves are usually quite prepared to accept them if they have something useful to offer. The story is told of an Oxford academic who was invited to deliver a lecture at Ruskin, the Oxford trade union college, and who began with the typically donnish, self-deprecating ploy of claiming to know very little of the subject in question. A voice from the back boomed out in a rich Lancashire accent: 'Tha'art paid to knoow!' It would be odd to turn up for a job at the pithead and claim archly that one knew awfully little about how to mine coal.

Ruskin students did not pull their punches. Some of them did a course in English literature, run at the time by a rather respectable Scottish woman, and there was a seminar on Blake's poem about a sick rose. Having read out the poem a little mincingly, the tutor asked her pupils what they thought it might mean. In most other colleges in Oxford, this would have been an invitation to reflect aloud on the intricate interweaving of the poem's various motifs, the hauntingly ambiguous nature of its imagery, the way it was hospitable to a number of divergent readings. But not at Ruskin. One hulking Scouser raised his hand and declared emphatically: 'It's VD, innit?' He might well have been right. But Ruskin students of literature tended to be hostile to the kind of Marxist literary theory some of us were practising down the road. The world of political power and material production was exactly what they had come to Oxford to escape, and reading novels and poems was a blessed respite from its rigours. Most of them were not interested in social interpretations of literature, any more than a medic would ponder the physiological aspects of kissing while out on a date.

We spent a good deal of time leafleting at the local car plant, never the most fruitful of activities. I would rise as the dawn seeped through my curtains, collect a comrade, now a distinguished Indian economist, and drive us both down to the factory to distribute leaflets as the early morning shift arrived in. The leaflets were not vapid propagandist stuff but contained detailed information, gleaned from comrades inside the plant, about the management's latest disreputable efforts to speed up work and hold back wages. Some of the workers knew this, and would even make a detour to collect a leaflet; others would tell us to fuck off back to Moscow, where (as they correctly pointed out) we would enjoy no such freedom of expression. One scrawny young Scot with a ginger goatee would spit in the proffered leaflet with such superb dexterity that his saliva would land plumb in the centre of it. Another lackey of the boss class once neatly stubbed his cigarette out in one as he dashed through the factory gates, leaving me with a fistful of hot ash.

After having thus sought to unfold the solution to the riddle of history, my colleague would go off to attend to his baby daughter, while I would go off to give a tutorial on Dickens or T. S. Eliot. At least we were not petty-bourgeois enough to go back to bed. It seemed a strange disjunction between theory and practice, the unity of which was much vaunted by the group. One comrade told me rather sanctimoniously that he 'derived his theory from his practice', by which he doubtless meant that he had arrived at his assessment of Rosa Luxemburg's theory of imperialism by selling newspapers outside Woolworth's every Saturday morning. I, by contrast, was an activist by conviction rather than temperament, and would most certainly have preferred reading Proust to picketing. I admired the gruellingly hard-work of other group members, and felt the lack of such dedication in myself; but after a while I came to realize that some of the group needed picketing just as much as I needed Proust, and that their conscientious devotion was thus not quite as selfless as it seemed. Left organizations often provide a social life for those who might otherwise find it hard to have one, and even early-morning leafleting is preferable to lying solitarily in bed all morning.

There were thus comrades who not only argued over politics, but ate, drank and slept them. Particularly slept. At one point in the group's career, venereal infections were circulating almost as rapidly as theories of neo-colonialism. Erection and insurrection became giddyingly confused, and the organization was like a cross between a commune and a harem. It provided a kind of cross-class dating service, by which weedy Glaswegian workers who couldn't believe their luck could hook up with frisky young women from Cheltenham Ladies' College with meticulously roughened-up accents. Paunchy, balding shop stewards found themselves to their astonishment as glamorous as rock stars in the eyes of young women fresh from convent school and anxious to compensate for their class crimes. Middle-class men competing with working-class colleagues for sexual favours from female members would obediently back off, acknowledging the historical priority of the proletariat. Other members were simply too hard-pressed with political work to have sex at all, or even to exchange erotic glances. The occasional couple snatched time from organizing jumble sales to have a baby.

It was babies, in fact, which almost split the group down the middle. Members regularly baby-sat for those comrades who had children, but this was an *ad hoc* sort of business, distinctly low in priority. Then some women in the group formally proposed that baby-sitting should become a compulsory duty for everyone. The leadership greeted the proposal with dismay: it was difficult enough recruiting a militant young car worker without breaking to him the distasteful news that he would have to take time off from smashing the bosses to sterilize bottles and warm up milk. But the women's motion carried the day, and a group which used to snigger at the use of the unisex word 'firefighter' had made a mildly historic turn.

They would perhaps have sniggered less had their classical etymology been up to scratch. The word *proletarius* in the ancient world meant those who were too poor to serve the state by property, and who served it instead by manufacturing labour-power. Their role was to produce children; and since the historical burden of this task has fallen more on women than on men, it is no mere modish gesture to claim that the proletariat is a woman. If that was so in antiquity, it is equally true today. The geographer David Harvey speaks of the oppositional forces of today's political world as the 'feminized proletariat'. Those dreary old bickerings between feminists and socialists still have their point; but they are being made progressively redundant by advanced capitalism itself. It is capitalism which is throwing socialists and feminists into one another's arms. One speaks, of course, metaphorically.

It was the police, rather than global capitalism, who once pitched me into the arms of a female comrade. The two of us had been pasting up posters in the city centre advertising a political meeting, and we were sitting in my car with our brushes and pots of paste, preparing to venture forth again. At that moment an inquisitive police car nosed its way out of a side-street. Police officers were under orders to keep illicit posters on their patch down to a reasonable level, and this police vehicle was clearly suspicious. Without a word, the two of us threw ourselves into a passionate clinch, and the police, seeing only a snogging couple, moved on. History had summoned us to set aside our natural modesty to further its august cause.

A right-wing newspaper once decided to do an exposé of the group. It turned out to be an admirably professional, scrupulously accurate job. Two men arrived in Oxford, put up for a fortnight at the poshest hotel in town, and proceeded to take us mercilessly apart. When we refused to open our front doors to them, they would shout through them bits of vital information which only four or five comrades, all of them as sound and loyal as Batman's butler, could conceivably have known. Anything which we committed to the post they had read within a day. A photographer popped up and tried for some shots of one of our senior members; when he was duly upbraided, he pulled a gun. The newspaper later admitted over the phone that he was a freelancer whom they used occasionally on 'delicate' cases. The two investigators doorstepped me a couple of times, dangling before my face a copy of a document which I had written for the group's eyes only. One of them was a crumpled Lunchtime O'Booze figure, while the other looked very much like a cop. With an air of genuine interest, he asked me to explain to him the difference between our group and another left organization over a highly esoteric point of Marxist doctrine. 'Oh, come on,' I protested. 'Your readers don't want to hear about that.' 'I know that,' he replied, 'but I do – honest I do. I've been studying this stuff for twenty years. What *is* the difference between you lot and the WRP on the transition from feudalism to capitalism?' He was evidently one of MI5's experts on historical materialism, and like some member of the Vice Squad assigned to destroying pornographic videos had developed a private taste for the stuff. I thought of starting with Hegel, but decided to slam the door on his foot instead.

I arrived at Oxford to find student militancy in full swing. Since I had free telephone facilities in college, unshaven students in trenchcoats would burst suddenly into my room during a tutorial on George Eliot and ask if they could phone Cuba or Mozambique. They would mutter a few coded, garbled words down the phone, then dash enigmatically out again. I gave a seminar in candlelight in the student-occupied Schools building on the High Street, the university proctors having craftily cut off the electricity supply. There were codes, signals, combat jackets, passwords, pseudonyms, all the panoply of a guerrilla army deployed to the end of obtaining a central students' union with snooker facilities. Students agitated for reform to the English Literature syllabus to chants of 'Remember Che!' I arrived at a radical Danish university to deliver a political lecture only to be met by two rather shamefaced-looking academics, one of them clutching a small tape-recorder. They explained to me with shyly lowered eyes that their students regarded lectures as a form of violence, but that if I would consent to speak into the tape-recorder, they would bear my recorded reflections away to the student body, who would then no doubt take a vote on whether they should listen to them or whether tape-recording was a form of technological oppression.

The student movement, then, had its minor absurdities. But it also played a vital part in ending a bloody war in south-east Asia, and in democratizing an academia which was criminally complicit with that violence. Better a wariness of tape-recorders than the smugness of a later generation of brutally self-interested young fogeys who knew from the age of eighteen precisely which desk in the Treasury they intended to occupy. In the Thatcherite years, reading a university subject like English, which brought with it no obvious entrée to the world of stockbroking, became an implicitly political option. Some students, at least, were still choosing to do what they enjoyed, in defiance of the crass utilitarianism around them, and Chaucer or Jane Austen accordingly took on a fresh political significance. But the intellectual climate had shifted drastically: twenty-year-olds who only a few years previously had moved in a milieu in which radicalism, even if they did not endorse it themselves, made as much sense as Darwinism or polio inoculations now gazed wonderingly on academics rumoured to be Marxists with the curiosity of someone encountering his very first coprophiliac. For the first time in several decades, a student generation had nothing of political interest to remember. Adrift and amnesiac, they were trapped inside their own experience like a goldfish in its bowl.

It is worth asking why what made political sense previously no longer makes so much sense now. What exactly has changed? It is not, of course, that the capitalist system has softened up. On the contrary, it has become more pervasive, aggressive and triumphalist than ever. And this, precisely, is what has changed. It is a question of business as usual only more so. And in that sense, socialism has been defeated rather than invalidated. In a curious paradox, what makes it more relevant than ever is exactly the fact that it is so powerless, since its powerlessness is a sign that the system it opposes is dangerously out of control.

One of the examiners of my doctoral thesis was the historian E. P. Thompson, whom I knew a little in extra-academic circles. I entered the examination room to find him gazing moodily out of the window, his great leonine thatch of greying hair reflected like an antique helmet in the glass. He was a lithe, rangy, loose-jointed man with piercingly blue eyes, the lean, slightly ravaged, handsome face of an actor, and a taste for cheap cheroots. One of them dangled from his lips as he asked me in his faintly hoarse upper-class drawl if I knew who was in possession of the letters from the minor figure I had worked on in my thesis to William Morris. Stumped by this corker of a first delivery, I confessed that I did not. He then informed me that he was.

It was not the most auspicious of openings to a doctoral exam. He continued to brood his way moodily through the session, but I found myself preferring this to his more hearty posture. There could be a streak of wholesome, honest-to-goodness, scout-masterish bluffness about him, as well as a rhapsodic, theatrical, over-the-top strain, a sort of nervous irascibility and a touch of what Perry Anderson once wickedly yet accurately called 'arch jocoseness'. But I was moved that this genuinely great man had taken the trouble to plough his way through my doctorese, though not so moved as to consider inflicting the thesis on the world in the shape of a book. It had caused quite enough suffering as it was.

When in political doubt, the left intelligentsia throw a conference or launch a journal. There is nothing wrong with conferences, as long as one realizes that they are more anthropological rituals, at which the like-minded may gather for mutual recognition and consolation, than theatres for genuine learning. Conferences are liturgical celebrations, affirmations of solidarity, symbolic spaces for those who speak a language (whether of socialism or orthodontics) unintelligible to most of their fellow-humans, and who there-fore need from time to time to relax with those of their kind, as a cross-dresser might feel the gathering urge to withdraw from the world of the bank or bakery and ease into a pair of corsets.

Left conferences in particular have their compulsive rituals and elaborate codes. There is always the man or woman who noisily claims the title of Most Alienated Person in the Conference, as well as the Real-World-Out-There, prolier-than-thou participant who reminds his colleagues that all this highbrow talk is all very well but they may not have noticed that there's a world of real people out there who wouldn't understand a single bloody word that's been spouted in the whole of these three days and what exactly do they propose to do about *them*? Voicing the opinion that theory is pointless unless it issues directly in world-transforming action within the next four minutes is a reliably vote-catching move, and will always win you a ragged bout of righteous applause. Then there is the man who rises from the audience to inquire at interminable length why no woman is speaking, the answer being that they might well if only he would stop hogging the floor.

There is also the bogus questioner who unburdens himself of a complex verbal treatise, putting an interrogative inflec-tion into his final words. And there is the chronically out-raged type, who never ceases to proclaim his disgust and moral revulsion at aspects of the system he nonetheless believes are historically inevitable. What you will not find at such gatherings is the most dispiriting stereotype of all: the militant young leftist who has matured with age into a sceptical liberal or stout conservative. Sheer horror of the cliché, if nothing else, has preserved me from this fashionable fate. Raymond Williams was further to the left when he died in 1988 than he was when I first met him in 1961.

Those who speak regularly at conventions know just how unfathomable is the human capacity for misinterpretation. If your title is 'Why We Must Smash Fascism', and your speech one luridly impassioned invective against it, there will always be somebody in the audience who will want to know why you are so soft on fascism. The person who came in half an hour late will imperiously demand to know why you failed to make a point which you made in your second sentence, while someone else will wonder aloud why, if you're so anti-bourgeois, you wear a suit and spectacles rather than dressing in cowhide and peering at the world through home-made lenses cut from discarded Guinness bottles on an antique lathe. If your subject is the poetry of Northern Ireland, some aggrieved audience member will inquire why you have been so churlishly silent about *fin-de-siècle* Bavarian orthopaedics. There is the chairperson who will introduce you by saying that you need no introduction, and who will bring the session to a close with some cack-handed joke based on a phrase plucked from your talk. Thus, if you have been speaking of the redistribution of income, he will suggest with heavy heartiness that the audience now 'redistributes' itself to the bar; if you mentioned exploitation, he will propose sardonically that we 'exploit' our speaker no longer. These things are laws of nature, which no mere human agency can affect.

There will generally be someone who will approach you after the session to let you know how vividly he remembers your lecture on ergonomics in Damascus, even though you know nothing of the former and have never visited the latter. There was a time when I would occasionally be mistaken for Terry Jones of the Monty Python team, since we share a first name and an interest in literature, and people would jovially recall some rib-cracking antic of mine in *The Life of Brian*, stonily resistant to the suggestion that they had got the wrong man. I was once asked how long it had taken me to write *The Making of the English Working Class*. People press upon you pamphlets about the mating habits of wombats or offer you a cure for warts. To be a public lecturer is to occupy a symbolic role rather than a real-life one, and almost nothing you can do can shake this identification. You could ostentatiously don a false red nose and start to pull on a pair of sponge-rubber trousers while being talked at by some mildly obsessive type after a lecture, but it would almost certainly be blocked out. And there are also the genuinely disturbed, who describe to you the messages they are receiving on the radio which the CIA have installed somewhere between their liver and lower intestine.

As conferences go, the Modern Languages Association of America is in a class of its own, as twelve or fifteen thousand literary critics take over a whole complex of hotels. It is a unique sociological experience to be on an escalator with sixty other people all of whom know who Jane Eyre is. Security is tight, and I once found myself unable to get in to a paper I was giving. As Jacques Derrida speaks to the crowded ballroom of the New York Hilton about floating the signifier, gorilla-shaped guards frisk fresh-faced post-graduate students on the doors. The president of the association is allotted the Hilton penthouse, and has the privilege of occupying the bed in which, either consecutively or simultaneously, Madonna, Paul Newman, Mohammed Ali, Elizabeth Taylor and Brad Pitt have slept. It is an enviable reward for a lifetime of annotating Dante.

In the end, the gulf between radicals and conservatives runs deeper than politics. A radical is one who cannot overcome her astonishment that there are people in the world who believe, by and large, that this is *it*. Hard though it is to swallow, these liberal or conservative types imagine that what we see now is pretty much all we will ever get. The error of the ultra-leftist, by contrast, is to fantasize that after the revolution *everything* will be different – that we shall abolish paper napkins as well as private property, transform toothbrushes along with the National Health Service. This is a delusion; but at least it keeps open the possibility of a future as spectacularly different from the present as the remote past. It is no wonder that capitalism seeks to erase the past, since the past speaks of difference, and thus of the future.

Marx famously observed that history tends to repeat itself; and of nothing is this truer than announcements of the end of history. Such obituary notices have been issued a good many times from the New Testament to Hegel. The pronouncement of the death of history simply adds a bit more history to what we have already, helps to keep history on the hoof, and so turns out to be curiously self-undoing. One of the last expulsion orders served on history, or more exactly on ideology, was that of the so-called end of ideology movement of the 1950s. With Vietnam, Black Power and the student movement just round the corner, it proved a singularly inept prophecy. Since such a pronouncement has been repeated in our own time, we should recall that as Oscar

Wilde might have remarked, to be wrong about the end of history once is misfortunate, whereas to be wrong about it twice is sheer carelessness.

5

Losers

At breakfast one morning as a child, I began idly to dig a hole with my spoon in the thick rim of my porridge. My mother noticed what I was doing, and I waited for her to tell me to stop. It was not a household in which one did anything without a point, unless prayer is to be included in that category. We would no more have done something without a definite function than we would have knocked nails into each other's skulls just for the sake of it. To my surprise, however, my mother encouraged me to make the hole wider and deeper. Then she took the milk jug and poured milk into it. The hole was just a convenient way of pouring milk on my porridge. The playful turned out to be pragmatic after all. There had been no Proustian epiphany. My porridge was not my madeleine.

Poverty is not the best school for learning to savour things in themselves. It is in this sense that it is anti-aesthetic, not just because it is unpleasant. Our life at home was as bare as a gerbil's, without friends, trips, entertainment, social skills. As Flann O'Brien observed, we had to keep the wolf from the door to stop it getting out. Trips, entertainment and the like were either things we could not afford, or were offensive to the spirit of grim utility which being poor tends to foster. Not for everyone, however. We were miserably hard up, but also miserable, which does not necessarily follow. Lots of families around us were on their beam-ends yet seemed to have fun. And though the impoverished Carmelites down the road did not exactly have fun, they were not slaves to utility either. There was nothing particularly useful about never having a square meal. We did not enjoy ourselves partly because we had aspirations, which made being impecunious a lot worse. The notion of enjoying life for its own sake was as much a mystery to us as sado-masochism or hermeneutics.

We led a cowed, daunted existence, socially sophisticated enough to be conscious of our social inferiority. Our aim in life was to have the words 'We Were No Trouble' inscribed on our tombstones. A knock at the front door would send us scrambling in terror like the thump of an SS rifle-butt, so unaccustomed were we to visitors. The sparsely furnished house was like a Beckettian stage-set in which nothing ever happened, since we lacked the resources for eventfulness to occur. The present is made up largely of what failed to happen in the past; my present, anyway. Today I have fewer books than almost any academic I know, perhaps out of some childhood sense that possessions are superfluous clutter. The house was rented from an absentee landlord, one of those shadowy Dickensian ogres who never put in a physical appearance, but to whom my father would occasionally write requesting some minor repair. It was the only writing he ever did. After an insultingly long time, the landlord would reply without addressing my father as 'Dear'.

Sparseness breeds fantasy – partly by way of compensation,

partly because there is too little actuality for the mind to feed on. So the reverse side of the tedium and timidity, for the children if not for the parents, was extravagant anecdotes, exorbitant word-play, a life in which nothing was real if not rhetorically performed. Language was our edge over a lacklustre world. There were Irish uncles who could extemporize brilliant comic patter for hours while knocking a tune out of a busted mandolin, Walter Mittyish aunts and cousins who had never used language for the purpose of accurate communication for more than five minutes but who could unburden themselves of a superb story. But it was not a place to hang around in, and our parents tried to ease us out of it, with the animal's instinct to push its offspring out of danger. They themselves represented the danger they were warning us off.

It is no surprise, then, that I became an early champion of the aesthetic, the lavish gesture, the end-in-itself, in a fairly cerebral sort of way. It was all still underpinned by an authentic Northern meanness. Utility was the enemy, and its opposite was art. As an adolescent I was much taken with the Angry Young Men, later a lot of dyspeptic old right-wingers, and once delivered an impassioned, dishevelled denunciation of the Establishment at an inter-school debating society. Afterwards, a sixth-former from a nearby girls' school drifted up and asked me in an awed tone if I was an existentialist. She had a flat but dimplish face, with a dusting of freckles on her nose. I had just about heard of existentialism, in some vague connection with Gauloises and roll-neck sweaters, but knew nothing about it other than that it was exotic and subversive. I replied, however, that I was, in an enigmatic tone intended both to intrigue and to conceal my ignorance. She confided in me that she was too, and that she had an older friend, a male university student, who said yes to everything. I did not much like the sound of this yea-saying friend, but wondered to myself whether she said yes to everything too. I was just about to inquire when she murmured something which sounded like 'quite a treat', but which on reflection might have been '*acte gratuit*', and drifted off.

The contrast between my parents and my Walter Mittyish relatives was a version of the battle between the good and the fine. It is the good who will enter the kingdom, but the fine who make life worth living in the meanwhile. Justice is part of goodness; it is no more than giving others their due; but mercy – letting others go scot-free when they flagrantly don't deserve to – has a sort of grandeur of spirit about it. Giving in excess of what is demanded is another such fine gesture, though it is divided only by a thin line from the ridiculous. I once lived for a while in California, in an apartment across the corridor from a young American woman called Liz. She earned her living as some kind of out-worker for a photographic company, but this did not seem to earn her much of a salary, and the rent was high. She had the intangible air of someone who has spent some time in a psychiatric institution, though I never had any actual evidence of this. One day she mentioned that she had a horse, which happened to be desperately ill. She had never referred to this horse before, but now she maintained that it was her most cherished possession, and that its illness was driving her to distraction. I asked her where the horse was kept, since we lived in a built-up area, and she gestured vaguely into the middle distance. The horse urgently needed an operation, which would cost 500 dollars. She did not have the money, so I gave it to her. For her it was quite a treat, whereas for me it was more of an *acte gratuit.*

I did not do this because I particularly liked her, and certainly not because I believed her. Nor did I do it as a tight-lipped act of charity. It was rather that the act of giving her the cash seemed the only absurdity appropriate to her finely preposterous tale. It was a way of worsting her conning of me by capping it, raising it to the second power, responding to her fiction with the even more demented act of actually giving her the money. It made the matter of who was laughing at whom intriguingly ambiguous. On the other hand, it was remotely possible that her tale was true, in which case I could retrieve a nugget of rationality from my extravagance. After a decent interval had elapsed I inquired after the horse's health, and was told he was as well as could be expected, though there seemed a dim possibility of convalescence fees on the horizon. These too I silently resolved to pay should the issue arise, partly to see how long we could spin this fiction out. I asked with a mild touch of malice whether I might visit the horse in whatever might be the equine equivalent of a sickbed, but was informed that this was strongly inadvisable. I have no doubt that it was.

You can always use the act of giving to take a rise out of someone. A left-wing friend of mine, when stopped on the street by someone rattling a can for charity, is in the habit of peering suspiciously at the label on the can and asking gruffly: 'Is this a Marxist organization?' When warmly assured that it is not, he waves his hand dismissively, says, 'I'm sorry, in that case I can't contribute,' and passes on.

The good are aware that they must sacrifice such

superfluous beauties as wit and style to a greater cause. They must be prepared to appear gauche and obstinate, be chided as kill-joys or upbraided for high-mindedness. It would be interesting to know at what historical point virtue came to seem tedious, and the devil to have all the best tunes. The fine, for their part, know that despite their magnificence they are unreliable in a crisis, and do not do well on the ways-and-means committee. In the conflict between the good and the fine, the acolytes of Tolstoy and the disciples of Wilde, the good must win out when the chips are down, but only then. To be good is perfectly sufficient, but as Walter Benjamin might have remarked, it is not the kind of life which sets the angels' bodies burning with one passionate flame of praise before their Creator. For the angels are in love with the cunning and crookedness of the human mind, not just with the moral virtues; and though the fine sail perilously close at times to the demonic, there is much to be said for them.

The good are just, whereas the fine are forgiving. Forgiveness breaks the futile circle of tit-for-tat, disrupting the rigorous economy of come-uppance. With a cavalier gesture, it sets the strict exchanges of justice aside, and in doing so anticipates a death in which all odds will be struck even. That you were cheated won't matter then, so perhaps it shouldn't be allowed to matter now. Forgiveness is a grand Jamesian gesture, a fine flourish of excess. The man whose grandfather hailed from Ballyjamesduff knew this well. But the dead themselves cannot forgive. They cannot relieve us of our fury that they should have disappeared, leaving us to clear up the mess.

*

There was a lot of disease and disability at primary school. There was the boy who stammered like a sten-gun and keeled over now and then clutching his hysterically paralysed leg, and the boy with the most amazing acne, his face knobbled, pitted and cratered like a lunar landscape. Some of these pustular protuberances were grey and dead while others were still active and erupting, flushed with dull fire. There was also a boy who was rumoured to have scalded his genitals and was entirely hairless, like a pink mottled egg. Impetigo was rife because of poor hygiene, so that half the pupils sported encrusted yellow sores, daubed in some cases with gentian violet. We were a spindly, stunted, hollow-chested crew, like a chorus line from *Les Misérables*. For several days each month, as regular as menstruation, I was racked by asthmatic spasms, gagging on my own sputum, breathless and delirious with inflamed bronchial tubes. I probably sailed close to death once or twice, which would have saved some conservative literary critics a degree of dyspepsia some years later, but I was mercifully unaware of how easily my frenetic breathing could have ceased altogether. My mother, desperate for a remedy, tried everything from waking me at dawn to feed me raw garlic, which did not endear me to my schoolmates the next day, to dressing me in a frilly little undervest made out of chamois leather, which did not endear me to them either. Perhaps the next experiment would have been to tie the garlic round my neck, but we never ventured that far.

Instead, someone told my parents of a homeopathic clinic in Manchester which was famed for its miraculous cures. None of us knew what 'homeopathic' meant, and we were not in the habit of looking up dictionaries. I suspected that the word was vaguely rude, but this is because I was confusing it with 'homosexual', which I had read in the newspaper in connection with the trial for sodomy of an aristocrat. Though the meaning of this word was obscure to me too, it had clearly disreputable overtones. It was hard to see how someone could set up a medical institution in this, let alone that it could be used to cure asthma. It seemed odd that something for which people were sent to gaol could be openly practised in a clinic, but perhaps it depended on how you did it, or how often.

The clinic was a dingy-looking shack down a back street, run by a burly, bow-tied Scot with the faintly suspect name of John Brown. Perhaps the name was a double bluff. There was one nurse, or at least a woman dressed as a nurse, who I sensed was Mrs Brown but who was not advertised as such. The sessions cost a pound each, which an aunt who had just won fifty pounds on the pools offered to pay. I seemed to be the only patient, and would come on Saturday mornings to sit in a cubicle and sniff some foul-smelling gas, perhaps carbon dioxide, through a rubber tube. The gas would bring on a spectacular asthma attack, which was evidently the point. This did not mean that the treatment was failing, so Dr Brown triumphantly informed us, but that it was going well. The more alarming my paroxysms, the more savagely exultant he became. He would stand over me as I wheezed and writhed, murmuring 'Splendid, laddie' and 'Keep it up, son' in his gruff Scottish brogue. I ended up in hospital for three weeks, and I imagine John Brown ended up practising liposuction with a blow-torch down some back alley or altering the appearance of drug barons on the run from the police.

Both of my baby brothers had been dispatched to eternity by the National Health Service. One had his skull damaged in birth, and had he survived longer than his two or three days would probably have been severely disabled; the other was smeared by a harassed nurse with some ointment she had just used on a child with an infection. He took rather longer to die, and I remember being lifted up to look at him in his coffin, a tiny waxen doll with a plug of cotton-wool in his mouth. It was the cotton wool which fascinated me. Nobody would tell me what it was for.

As usual with the industrial working class, the talk was of the body, though not in the style of a California graduate seminar. Our elders rambled on endlessly about haemorrhoids and catarrh, prolapse and lumbago, cataracts and rheumatoid arthritis. We were the walking wounded of the industrial revolution, a Dad's army of adenoidal midgets. In common with most of the north-of-England working class, we were a good few inches below average height, like a herd of extras from *The Wizard of Oz*. Illness was feared, more for its social effects than its physical ones, but people took a grisly relish in it as well, since it was the only dramatic event that ever befell them. Nothing that happened in your daily life was likely to measure up to the majestic size of death or a major operation, which were the only real sources of narrative among us. Doctors were revered yet also resented, as a kind of alien wedge or middle-class fifth column in our midst, overbearing and sometimes brutish yet armed with the esoteric knowledge people needed to stay in work. The doctor, not the teacher or cleric or lawyer, was the only member of the middle classes who really mattered. And even the middle classes were not pukka middle classes, in the sense of speaking Standard English. Nobody spoke Standard English.

There were, however, traces of a more patrician group around the place, enigmatic signs which referred to a secret society or upper-class club known as the Patrons. These were so powerful, all-privileged a coterie that whole car-parks, cloakrooms, lavatories, bars, hat-racks and gardens throughout the city were set aside for their exclusive use, labelled 'Patrons Only' to deter us lesser breeds. Indeed, they seemed so exclusive that they made the Garrick look like Sheffield Wednesday Supporters' Club. I had never encountered a Patron in the flesh, but I imagined them as dim, silvery figures with white tapering fingers and resonant, cultivated voices. They seemed altogether too exalted a species to require such lowly facilities as lavatories and car-parks, but I suspected that their own versions of these affairs bore only a remote resemblance to our own – that their lavatories, for example, echoed to the strains of organ music mingled with the plashing of perfumed water into ruby-studded basins. Nowadays, though I still feel a faint quiver of intimidation when I spot a Patrons Only sign, I realize that some kindly soul might well have approached me when I stood as a child in some cinema queue and murmured into my delighted, astonished ear that I was a Patron too, rather as someone might break to a smelly vagrant sprawled on a park bench the enthralling news that he is the legitimate heir of the crown prince of Moravia.

All this perpetual narrative of suffering went on despite the fact that physical pain is a kind of meaninglessness, a brute fact as hard to make anything of as a sneeze. It is just something that happens to you, like belching or falling over your feet; and although there is much to be said about the outworks of it (time off work, hospital visits, saintly or savage nurses), as well as about its causes, location, duration, quality, intensity and potential cure, pain itself is so much the epitome of brute fact that it seems to slip through the nets of language. It is just not part of the order of meaning. It is rather a disruption of meaning, a garbling of sense, a sort of solipsism. It is part of the body's obdurate resistance to intelligibility, its blind, obtuse persistence in its own being. And if pain is meaningless, then so is much of the human history which is saturated by it. In the semiotics of suffering, the abolition of pain is a victory for meaning and a triumph over randomness, even if some postmodern theory sees such randomness, absurdly, as a kind of freedom.

There are, to be sure, creative kinds of meaninglessness too, those of the Fool or the Dadaist, and what seems scrambled at the time may always prove decodable later on. The jest is a piece of nonsense in the service of solidarity rather than isolation, but one which promotes fellow-feeling exactly by being an end in itself. It differs in this sense from the joke told by a superior to put you at your ease. But there is also that alternative universe which is as close to us as blood and breathing, that inconceivably different place known as agonizing pain into which every moment of our life is potentially a strait gate, and which seems too obscene even for the devil to have created. It is notable that the Jesus of the New Testament, who spends much of his time curing the sick, never once counsels anyone to reconcile himself to his sickness. On the contrary, he seems to associate illness with evil. He certainly seems to have panicked at the prospect of his own physical torture, if the garden of Gethsemane episode is anything to go by. It may be that unavoidable suffering can sometimes be turned to fruitful use, but this does not justify its existence. It would be far better if we had no such occasions for moral heroism.

The form which tries to convert suffering into value is known as tragedy. At the centre of traditional tragedy stands the tragic scapegoat, who is laden with the sins of the people, and having thus become monstrous and unclean is driven out into the wilderness. Thrust beyond all respectable social order, the disgusting embodiment of a trauma we dare hardly contemplate, the scapegoat wanders in a hellish realm of meaninglessness. In Christian terms, this is Christ's descent into hell after his scapegoating on the cross, the solidarity with human despair and destitution by which he 'becomes sin' for our sake. But it is also the blinded Oedipus and the demented Lear, all those violently disfigured creatures who have strayed beyond the frontier of the acceptably human into some ghastly limbo of life-in-death.

For the tragic vision, only by finding our own image in this terrible deformity can we be healed. We must come to pity what we fear, finding in this monstrous travesty of humanity the power to transfigure the human. For the liberal, there are no monsters, only those driven to violence by deprivation; for the conservative, monsters are other people; for the radical, the real monsters are ourselves. But they are also what the Old Testament calls the *anawim*, the dispossessed or shit of the earth who have no stake in the present set-up, and who thus symbolize the possibility of new life in their very dissolution. St Paul sees Jesus as a type of them.

Nobody can actually spend their days as a tragic scapegoat. There are no vacancies in it at employment centres. You cannot roam in a realm of the mad and meaningless while dropping the children off at school. There are more mundane forms of garbage than the *anawim* to be attended to. There is something inhuman about self-sacrifice, just as there is something inhuman about a certain sort of revolutionary. Self-sacrifice is no way to live. On the contrary, as Aristotle understood, virtue is all about having a good time.

How then could those Carmelites have believed that the model of how to live was Jesus? He was murdered! It is true that murderees are usually admirable people, if newspaper reports of them are anything to go by. Just as almost all apprehended murderers are said by their neighbours to be quiet types who 'kept themselves to themselves', so almost all accounts of murder victims emphasize how much they enjoyed life, were full of *joie de vivre*, bubbled and bounced with fun and couldn't do enough for others. People with these qualities ought to watch it when they walk alone at night. But the fact remains that the crucified are hardly an image of the good life. Not even the Carmelites thought that. Their image of the good life was heaven, which they were hardly obtuse enough to confuse with their own semi-destitute existence. Wherever heaven was, it was not in industrial Salford. They did not imagine that everyone could live like themselves, any more than dukes or circus clowns do. Living as a symbol is strictly a minority pursuit. For them, sacrificial victims like themselves were tragically necessary only as long as the world was as it is.

My father's life had the unattractiveness of the victim. Like many a parent, he sacrificed himself for his children, but that made him precisely not a model to emulate. If we children need to make sacrifices too, there would have been no point in his. Sacrificial fathers are no fun, though without their sacrificing you might never get to have much fun yourself. He was a deeply intelligent man, who had won a place at the local grammar school but had to pass it up, as his family could not afford the fees or uniform. He was one of twelve children of Irish immigrant parents, who, rather astonishingly, had eloped together to England from Tipperary. Romantic moonlight flits could hardly have been the sociological norm in late nineteenth-century Roscrea. All fourteen of them lived in a tiny terraced house in a Salford slum, but it was a point of pride with them that nobody slept downstairs. Instead, most of the children slept in the rafters, as they sometimes did in the traditional Irish cabin.

In this way, the 'parlour' or downstairs front room could be kept sacrosanct. The working-class parlour is a sort of equivalent to the upper-class drawing-room, a leisurely place where you can smoke your cigars, play bridge or engage in civilized conversation. But since the working class does none of these things, the parlour is kept empty, as a kind of witness to the fact that you have neither time, training nor inclination for such pursuits. Just as the tomb of the unknown soldier is significant because no one knows who is inside it, so the parlour has meaning because nothing goes on there. It is 'kept for best', but since the best never happens it remains a shell.

There was a distinction between my father and my mother's family, painfully apparent to us but no doubt utterly invisible to the eye of a middle-class beholder. My father's family were lower working class, while my mother's people were upper working class; and though both of my grandfathers worked as labourers in the local gasworks, for them this was quite as momentous a divide as the one between landed and industrial capital. It was like some nuance of tint vividly present to the eye of a sloth but concealed from the vision of the zoologist. My mother's mother had worked as a barmaid, but she came from a small farm near Newry and had the icy contempt of the self-sufficient peasant for the dependent labourer. An Irish rural distinction was thus grafted on to the streets of industrial Lancashire. She hardly noticed the girls of the family; girls would not inherit the farm, and the fact that there was no farm in the middle of Salford to inherit did nothing to modify this prejudice.

My grandmother combined working-class poverty with petty-bourgeois values, and so was afflicted with the worst of both worlds. She was a consummate actress, who with one flicker of her sorrowful, cow-like eyes could reduce a whole roomful of merry-makers to the most atrocious spasms of guilt. She appeared to be the archetypal, long-suffering, don't-mind-me-I'll-make-do-with-a-scrap-of-badger-droppings Irish mother, though this concealed a self-centredness which would have put Caligula to shame. Her fantasy, I imagine, was to hobble painfully down the street in her best overcoat, wallowing along like a trusty old tug, while from behind a hundred rubber plants and lace curtains neighbours peered out to murmur with caught breath: 'There's Mrs Tierney on her way to daily Mass, God knows how she manages it on them legs.'

The legs in question were a central part of my childhood mythology, as numinous an object as the bow of Philoctetes or the shield of Achilles. She had been run over by a grocer's van, but though her injuries were relatively mild, she responded to the event as though she had been fed through a sausage machine or dropped from a great height into a tankful of sharks. She won herself a spot of legal compensation for the accident, but kept it quiet partly in case her poverty-stricken children asked her for a share of the money, and partly because being compensated might tarnish her tragic status. The accident was in a way no more than poetic justice. Some years earlier in Ireland, her brother had run over the local midwife in his horse and cart, drink, as the Irish say in the passive voice, having been taken. The midwife was killed on the spot, but I doubt there was any compensation, or indeed much involvement of the state at all, the Irish attitude to colonial law (as it was at the time) being admirably casual.

Everything in this family was done nudgingly, back-handedly, on the sly. My grandmother looked a little like a cross-dressed version of the poet Seamus Heaney – they both hailed from rural Ulster, possibly from the same gene pool – and believed with Heaney's folk that whatever you said you should say nothing. No doubt being brought up a Catholic in a sectarian Protestant state had a lot to do with it, though in my grandmother's case one could add a large dose of demonic perversity. The resemblance between her and Heaney was physical only, since she was hardly a dab hand at prolepsis or litotes. She was fly, close, arch, underhand, as pious as a postulant and as devious as a diplomat, and would have made a superb Jesuit. Instead, lacking the genital and educational requirements for such a role, she became a kind of clerical groupie, and the idea that a priest would speak well of her to others yielded her a supreme, almost libidinal pleasure. I imagined her enticing the local clergy into her parlour with the bait of a free cup of tea, hypnotizing them with her mournful, cow-like eyes, then standing over their immobilized forms hissing 'Mrs Tierney's a good woman' over and over into their spellbound ears, until they were sent dazed and reeling into the streets to chant this mantra obediently to all and sundry. She was once mortified to find a priest walking behind her on the pavement when her stockings were not of the cleanest, and remarked to my mother that 'If Father had known who I was, he would have said "That can't be Mrs Tierney"', an intellectual conundrum one may leave to the logicians to unravel. My mother was as terrified of her as a victim of her torturer, and remained so long after she died.

She never spoke to my father's people, though they lived only a street away, and she despised them as tribal and unhygienic, which indeed they were. She was also put out by the fact that my father's mother, who was genuinely rather than spuriously long-suffering, was known as the saintliest woman in Rockley Street, sainthood being a status to which she herself wickedly aspired. Since Rockley Street was hardly the length of Park Avenue, this was a somewhat backhanded compliment, rather like praising someone for being the best oboe player in the entire bathroom; but my grandmother resented the attribution of even averagely good intentions, let alone sanctity, to anyone but herself. She was able to find shoddy motives lurking behind others' good deeds with a dialectical subtlety which Hegel would have envied.

Besides, though my father's people were not at all feckless, neither were they respectable. My maternal grandmother, by contrast, was respectable working class, and in coming across from County Down she had also come down. My father thus married above himself, though by the slimmest of social gradations, and was always conscious of the fact. He would stress his respect rather than his affection for my mother, as though she were some sort of Southern belle and he was an extraordinarily fortunate hillbilly. Yet his parents could read and write, having been taught by the monks in Roscrea, whereas my mother's father was illiterate. My mother's mother was only slightly more gifted in the literary realm. She once sent me a note when I was in hospital which ended 'Terry, you are a better writer nor me', a self-referential utterance worthy of a French symbolist.

Whereas a middle-class man would wear his cap out of doors and smoke his pipe in the house, my mother's father wore his cap in the house and smoked his pipe out of doors. In the back yard, in fact, to where my grandmother would banish him along with a malodorous mongrel. He wore a cravat round his neck as a middle-class man might, but a middle-class man would no doubt have worn a shirt with it. He could be dewy-eyed about Ireland, and once described it to me with caught breath as 'sacred soil'; yet his memories of the place seemed blurred and probably for the most part thoroughly unpleasant, and he had not the slightest intention of ever returning. Since the Salford gasworks was scarcely utopia, this said quite a bit about wherever it was he had left behind.

There was no real relationship between him and my grandmother. Relationships were for those who could afford them. The Ireland they grew up in was still a place of dowries and matchmakers. One of her sons, who blarneyed and charmed his way from working in a biscuit factory to lecturing in a polytechnic, toured the Salford pubs as 'Prince of Crooners'.

We were a family of performers rather than achievers. My own eldest son, despite being born with only one arm, used to earn his living by juggling. Another uncle, despite his midget-like appearance, had been something of a boxer in the navy, and would disappear every now and then for a few days' boozing. When he finally turned up to confront his exasperated wife, he would shadow-box maniacally around her, gesturing boisterously to his chin and bawling, 'Stick one on 'ere, Connie, go on, stick one on 'ere!' He needed his binges, though: he had served in the submarines during the war, evolutionarily adapted to the role by his dwarfish height, and my aunt would sometimes wake up at night to find him crouched over the armchair in the parlour, screaming like a baby.

What I remember most of my father is silence. He was silent because he was agonizingly inarticulate, and deeply ashamed of it. One failure of speech thus overlaid another. He was cut off from communication, lacking language to excess. Perhaps I have compensated enough for that in my time. I am still not sure whether his silence was a rock or an abyss, strength or indifference. He was painfully shy and unsociable, yet also practical, rational, reliable and infinitely patient. He could do quite advanced mathematics by some home-spun system of his own, without having been trained in it at all, and had he been properly educated he would have made an excellent engineer. He was always inventing things in his mind: a packet of crisps complete with a small sachet of vinegar, a bed which would slope upwards to rest your legs. He did not think much of artistic types like me.

After thirty-odd years in an engineering factory, he drew his paltry pension and bought an off-licence in a slum area of Salford which was already being demolished. The cellar was slimy with snails, drawn there by the beer. They were certainly more drawn to the beer than was my father, a devout teetotaller. Perhaps I compensated for him in that way too. The shop was the fulfilment of his dream to be his own 'gaffer' or boss. But the dream was only to survive for a couple of years. We shall burn that bridge when we come to it.

There are two images of God. One is as Judge, before whom we seek to bargain our way to salvation by performing certain cultic rites and being remarkably well-behaved. This is the God of the pharisees and patriarchs, for whom if it isn't unpleasant it can't be virtuous, and his Old Testament name is Satan, which in Hebrew means something like 'accuser'. The other image of God is of he who does not need to be appeased because he has forgiven us already, and scandalously accepts us just as we are. This image of God, as counsel for the defence or even as co-defendant in the dock, is known as Jesus, friend of the shit of the earth. It is one of the more grisly ironies of the Christian gospel that when God finally got round to putting in a disgracefully belated appearance in the world he had created, he did so as a political criminal. This God is largely hostile to family values, has almost nothing to say about sexuality, and demands that we love strangers as much as we love our kinsfolk.

I was familiar all my childhood with the love of strangers. Because my father never broke his silence, it was hard to know whether he was a friend or an alien. Was he counsel for the defence, or a Nobodaddy? He bored his workmates with tales of how well we were doing at school, but never once praised us to our faces. He did not touch us or play with us; nothing in his own impoverished upbringing had taught him how. It was the old working-class suspicion of softness. It was a bleak world out there, and you did not unfit your children for it by teaching them a lot of airs and graces. Love was a question of doing, not of feeling. Catholics did not go in for all that subjective mush.

6

Dons

I stumbled through Cambridge sick at heart. It was as though I had murdered to get in. In my undergraduate years, the early 1960s, almost all the students seemed well over six foot tall, the products of centuries of good breeding, brayed rather than spoke, and addressed each other in stentorian tones in intimate *tête-à-tête* conversation. One is tempted to add that the men were just the same, in the manner of the old joke; but in fact at that time there were hardly any women students at all. These chinless young blades stamped their feet and hooted in cinemas at the feeblest of jokes, and elbowed the cowed townspeople off the thin medieval pavements. My room-mate, who was occasionally audacious enough to wear jeans, was pulled in by his Tutor and asked sharply why he dressed like a garage mechanic. In Hall, people spoke as though they had hot potatoes in their mouths even when they didn't. Nobody puked their beetroot over the table.

I spent my second year renting a room in the home of a man who was a steward or butler at one of the colleges. He must have been a glutton for upper-class patronage since he was also a university bulldog, which is to say a top-hatted assistant to the proctors or university disciplinary officers.

In those days we were required to wear our gowns in the streets of Cambridge after dusk, to distinguish us from the local rabble, and the proctors, flanked by their trusty bull-dogs, would patrol the town centre and fine any student whom they caught improperly dressed. A friend of mine was so daunted by this prospect that he even wore his gown in public lavatories, to the raucous jeers of the young townsfolk standing at his elbow. If you were caught on the street you could make a run for it to a college if you had the nerve, since the proctors' jurisdiction ended there; but if you chose this course the bulldogs might give chase, and if they caught you you were in trouble. Myth had it that one of the bulldogs was chosen for speed and the other for stamina. I lived in dread of being chased down the street by my own landlord, imagining the deathly silence at breakfast next morning.

My landlord was a surly, stammering character with a brutal head, a rogue eye and sinisterly magnifying spectacles, a working-class fascist who fawned on those above him and bullied those below. He had, as Brecht remarked of such types, the posture of a cyclist, crouching low and treading hard. My presence was therefore bound to plunge him into ontological crisis, since though I was a 'grad', as the locals called us, I was clearly no better socially than I should be, and certainly no better than him. I thus provided an unwit-ting focus for his pathological class-ambivalence, incarnating his inner turmoil to the point where he could hardly bear to have me in his house but could ill afford not to. He detested me for not allowing him to relish his resentment by being someone he could cringe to. Just being under his roof was enough to remind him how hard-up he was, an outrage which I might at least have assuaged by knocking him around a bit with a lordly air, or receiving mail with 'Rt. Hon.' on the envelope. It seemed unfair to use his lavatory without adding a touch of class to his place in return for the privilege. His shrivelled, mad-eyed wife would look piteously at me over his shoulder, as if mutely imploring me to arrange for her a helicopter and a rope ladder. It was her second marriage, and once, in a fit of gross indiscretion, she told me that my landlord 'wasn't worth the little finger' of her first husband. Even without having met her first husband, it was hard to disagree.

After a series of grotesque contretemps, I managed to get a room in college and thought myself free of this monster for good. But I had reckoned without the degree ceremony, where his role was to check that we candidates for graduation were properly attired in our gowns, black suits and white bow ties. I could see him in the middle distance, working his way methodically along the rows of students, adjusting a collar here and the hang of a gown there, and even, I think, gravely raising the odd bushy beard to ensure that it concealed a stipulatory bow tie. I was half-expecting him to ignore me when he finally arrived before me, given the acrimony with which we had parted; but I had reckoned without his genetic obsequiousness. Instead of kneeing me painfully in the groin while pretending to smooth my lapel, he broke into a delighted smile and shook my hand warmly. He had obviously heard that I had done well in the exams, and was already busy rewriting our narrative in more comic or chivalric mode. I could not hiss at him, as I had half intended to do, that he was a loathsome little turd, since he had escaped into amnesia. The amnesiac cannot be forgiven, since they have forgotten that they have offended.

My supervisor, Dr Greenway, had a private income and a fine old house just outside the town, where he was served by a Spanish butler and a Spanish maid. Sometimes, after a supervision, he would glance conspiratorially around his enormous study, lower his voice confidentially, and murmur: 'I say, would you like to come to lunch with me next Wednesday?' It was said in the nervous, sidelong manner of a seducer, and one imagined a soulful *tête-à-tête* in some discreetly opulent restaurant. But the invitation would be to his house, and you would arrive there to find about forty other students milling round, all of them presumably recipients of the same hushed, wheedling request, and all no doubt secretly waiting for the moment when the other guests would be dismissed and the *tête-à-tête* would begin. Greenway would place himself at the head of a table as long as an airport runway, and cry, 'Major scholars!' Those undergraduates with major scholarships would move to the seats beside his, while Greenway cried out again: 'Minor scholars!' Then the minor scholars would sidle to their seats rather lower down the table, followed in due course by the exhibitioners. Finally, the commoners would be invited to herd and grovel below the salt, almost as far out of Greenway's earshot as Niagara Falls. They were so far away that it was hard to see whether they were supplied with cutlery or not, or whether they were left to eat with their hands.

Greenway was the first truly civilized man I had ever encountered, and about as warmly spontaneous as a shaving brush. He knew all about cheeses, wisteria, Rubens's brushwork, herbaceous borders, flying buttresses, gilt-edged securities, the bird-life of Venezuela, varieties of Malaysian fruit, Leibniz, Gregorian chant, brandy, the law of tort, the manufacture of saddles, seventeenth-century military strategy, water-colours, breeds of North African dog, the vowel-sounds of Afrikaans, the vegetation of the Minho valley. All this knowledge seemed as built-in as his pancreas, or at least effortlessly acquired, and having just arrived at university I began to understand that education was not really to be acquired from books. It was rather like joining the army only to be instructed that firearms were morally despicable. Or rather, knowledge could no doubt be culled in this way, but something more precious, known as cultivation, could not. That one picked up as one did typhoid or a charming new acquaintance, but it could not be learnt any more than you could learn how to sneeze or have an erection. Cultivation also taught you at what angle to wear your knowledge, how loose or tight or tilted to let it sit on you, which was almost as important as what you knew.

It was my first glimmering of difference between erudition and intelligence, which I had always imagined went together. Greenway was certainly intelligent, but he had no more ideas in his head than a hamster. Indeed, he was not only bereft of ideas but passionately opposed to them, which struck me as a little odd for a doctor of philosophy. He did not see the need for them, any more than he saw the need for wrapping his feet in asbestos or wearing a tutu. I soon discovered that his role as a teacher was to relieve me of my ideas, as the role of a burglar is to rifle your bedroom. I would stagger into a supervision clutching a huge, unwieldy armful of them, and he would cut them briskly down to size, toss them dismissively to each side and pack me off poor but honest. If we were discussing, say, Hume's theory that reason is always a slave of passion, he would say something like 'It all depends on the individual', as though we were talking about a taste in broccoli. He seemed to think that whether space was curved or rabbits had concepts depended on the individual too. He was a naturally astute character, but ideology had rendered him obtuse, like some gradual wasting of the brain. He was as allergic to ideas as a wrestler or a stock-broker. If you had presented him with a text containing the secret of the universe, he would have noticed only a displaced semi-colon. It did not do to be too clever, and the trick was to find a way of speaking about Heraclitus or John Stuart Mill which Princess Margaret might understand.

As a student, Greenway had mainly studied philosophy, not English, which was not at the time considered a drawback to being the senior Fellow in English at a Cambridge college. He had read English literature rather as he had visited the Prado or picked up the rules of croquet, and he was hardly incapable of whiling away a pleasant hour talking about Jane Austen. When we did discuss Austen's fiction, his comment on the rival suitors of the heroine of *Mansfield Park* was: 'Well, personally I wouldn't marry either of them.' Even then, I had the uneasy feeling that literary criticism was supposed to involve a little more than this, though exactly what I wasn't sure. It seemed the kind of thing that Princess Margaret might say, which was surely not why I had amassed all those A levels. He once told me that someone had rung him up when he was sitting in his rooms in the Inns of Court and asked him whether he would like the Trinity English Fellowship. I take it that he had said yes, as someone might say yes to the offer of a glass of whisky. So he had been a lawyer as well, though it was unclear quite where he had fitted that in. I would not have been particularly surprised to learn that he was also a botanist or a Sanskrit scholar. All these things, in those days at least, seemed to depend more on who than what you knew. Professional training came in handy, but it was not indispensable. A firm grounding in the classics was probably thought sufficient qualification for becoming a brain surgeon.

He sometimes lectured on ancient Greek tragedy, trawling through a text line by line in a dry monotone but occasionally peering excitedly at the lectern, as though he had just spotted a exotic insect nestling on his book, exclaiming in a tone of mounting urgency: 'Just a minute, there's a crux (textual problem) here!' This was the nearest he ever approached to human drama, though he was capable of some unsettling gestures. Sometimes, during our supervisions, he would pull a nasal inhaler out of his waistcoat pocket and stick it violently up his nose. His flaring, imperious eyes would continue to hold my glance at these moments, as though mutely daring me to make some comment on this action. He suffered from the dank Fenland climate, and from time to time would speculate aloud at our sessions about leaving Cambridge and going elsewhere. But he would do this in the playful, semi-jocose tones of a man contemplating something he knew was utterly absurd or logically impossible, like taking a day-trip to Saturn or sprouting a pair of antlers. One could as well imagine him anywhere other than Cambridge as one could imagine the Dalai Lama in a strip joint. The idea of him in Houston or Huddersfield was grotesque.

Indeed, during my years in Oxbridge, I came to see that the place was full of people who were there largely because they could not conceivably be anywhere else, as some people can only be in top-security psychiatric institutions or houses with views of the English Channel. There is a kind of lumpen intelligentsia in Oxbridge who have no real jobs but who, as in some Buñuel-like fantasy, find themselves incapable of leaving, as long-term prisoners grow gradually more terrified as the fatal moment comes for them to rejoin the world. Oxbridge colleges, like hospitals and monasteries, have an infantilizing effect on their longer-term inmates, reducing them to a state of querulous narcissism. I knew of a don at Cambridge who bought his cigarettes from a machine – not because he approved of soulless modern machinery, but because the thought of human contact over a counter was even more distasteful to him. If Oxbridge was closed down, the Greenways – nowadays, thankfully, a rare, exotic species – would have to be herded on to special reservations where they could continue to receive their special High Table diet, protected by high fences from the jeering importunity of the mob, who would be allowed to photograph them only at appointed times.

Greenway did not stoop to much research, though he produced the odd pedantic little edition. He had an astonishing range of knowledge, but no idea at all how to use it. He was like a gardener glumly contemplating a mound of vegetables he had planted which was now darkening the sky, wondering what on earth to do with them all. I heard later of an antique Cambridge don who worked in a small department which had just acquired a new, zealous head who insisted that his colleagues produce some tangible evidence of research. In the Cambridge of those days, this would no doubt have been as stunning a demand as requiring the dons to have sexual intercourse in public with sheep. Publication was in general regarded as a mildly vulgar, publicity-seeking

affair, as opposed to more enduring achievements like providing some robust chairmanship of the college wine committee. The new head of department, fed up of having to
chivvy his laggard colleagues, eventually set them a deadline
for producing their research, and as the hour of reckoning
drew nearer, the ancient don grew more and more visibly
agitated. Finally, at ten minutes to midnight on the deadline
day, the window of his house in a leafy Cambridge suburb
was heard to open, and his quavering voice rang out across
the street: 'Stop thief! He's got my research!'

Greenway lived an extraordinarily privileged life. I once
arrived late at a supervision with him, explaining that I had
had to walk back from the dentist. He did not seem to grasp
the meaning of this sentence at all, and I realized after a
while that for him the idea of visiting a dentist in Cambridge,
rather than in London, was as astonishing as if I had told
him that I regularly visited the ladies' lavatory or a brothel
specializing in dwarfs. He seemed to think that I might as
well fill my own teeth as allow a local dentist to do it. A
friend of mine, a fellow student, was once sitting talking to
him in his study when the room began to grow cold. There
was a small electric fire, its switch a foot or so from
Greenway's armchair, but he did not turn it on. Instead, he
crossed the room, lifted his telephone, and summoned a
college servant to switch it on for him.

It was not that he was indolent; why in that case get up
from his chair? Nor was he in the least high and mighty, and
he did not seem to enjoy ordering people around. On the
contrary, he had the courtesy, decency and self-effacement
of the genuine patrician, rather than the domineering style
of the socially insecure. It was just that he had been brought

up to believe that manual work was what servants did, and he would no more have thought of doing it himself than he would have thought of extracting his own appendix. It was not a matter of pride or principle; it was just the way things were. He once described his gardener to me as 'the salt of the earth', without any sense that this was as dreary a cliché as 'the men are getting restless' or 'it's a fair cop'. 'All stout fellows,' he once remarked to me of the college porters, though he confided his doubts about one, a Welsh socialist, who refused to tip his bowler hat to him. He would have shrunk fastidiously from clichés like 'at the end of the day' or 'a dreadful silence fell over the room', but when it comes to the issue of class even subtly intelligent liberals can lapse into banality.

And Greenway was not a liberal. I once had a chat with his English-rose, jolly-hockey-stick-type secretary, in the course of which she wondered aloud what his politics might be. This said as much about her politics as his, since cudgelling one's brains over his political views would be rather like regarding the ethnic origin of Louis Armstrong as a baffling mystery. But though he was not a political liberal, preferring order to freedom and espousing a fierce anti-egalitarianism, he represented my first furtive, fumbling, adolescent encounter with the liberal mind. I was an eighteen-year-old working-class Catholic, as certain as a speak-your-weight machine and as ignorant as a fish; he was a middle-aged patrician who knew an enormous amount but made a virtue out of agnosticism. I was an enthusiast of the pure ice, whereas he was a denizen of the rough ground. He seemed to derive an almost erotic *frisson* from not knowing what he thought, and would conclude some discussion with a wry, mock-defeatist

'Oh, I don't know,' pitched somewhere between intellectual humility and cavalier insouciance.

This shocked my dogmatic sensibilities almost as much as if he had finished every sentence with a dismissive 'Oh, cock and balls.' Where I came from, there were all kinds of issues on which it was important to know where you stood, and not knowing was regarded as a deficiency rather than a virtue. But Greenway saw education more as an unfolding ignorance than an accumulating knowledge, and he was my first experience of those for whom truth is a fairly trifling affair. Today, they hang out on every English department corridor. For him, truth simply ground to a kill-joy conclusion the coruscating flash of mind upon mind, opinion on opinion. I rejected this at the time for the wrong reasons, but also for the right ones. The fact that he could afford to disregard how it was with the world, whereas others less privileged could not, hardly needed pointing out. Or rather, it needed pointing out only to the likes of him, as a piece of self-ignorance which underpinned his delight in ignorance. When he spoke in this fashion, I could see the Spanish maid and butler lurking dimly behind his discourse. Only later was I to learn that this was known as the doctrine of base and superstructure. Nobody I had ever met had amassed so much knowledge and been so little in need of it.

Greenway was not only a blue-blooded Tory, but almost certainly a recruiter for the British intelligence services. In earlier years the college had been the academic home of the Cambridge spy circle, and third-year students would still attend mysterious country-house parties in Sussex before disappearing into what was euphemistically called the Foreign Office. Those who combined intellectual talent with athletic prowess, a rare enough blend, were particularly prone to evaporate in this way. Greenway was not rash enough to try to enlist a truculent leftist like myself, but he made a stab at signing up a friend of mine who happened to mention to him one day that he had no idea what to do after graduating. 'Have you considered espionage?' Greenway inquired, in the off-hand tone of a man asking whether he had thought of trying a different brand of hair-oil. My friend, thinking this a rare outbreak of humour on Greenway's part, asked him banteringly whether it was dangerous. Greenway replied unbanteringly that it was.

He had rooms next to a well-known Marxist economist, who I liked to imagine was a recruiter for the KGB. Perhaps the two of them compared their day's tally over lunch. No doubt Greenway needed this swashbuckling stuff to bring a touch of adventure to what was otherwise a surreally sedate existence. He seemed to live literally by the book – in his case, a slim volume of college regulations known as the White Book. 'It's not in the White Book' was his constant refrain. One could imagine him intoning this phrase if someone tried to mug him, or if a lover proposed some risqué new sexual practice. It was not in the White Book to spit, fart, despair, over-enthuse, misidentify a cognac, subscribe to Hegel's theory of negation or forget to address one's supervisor as 'sir'. For part of our undergraduate years he was senior proctor of the university, a role which allures the legalistically-minded. Fortunately, I never ran into him after dusk without my gown, though had I done so I am sure he would have treated me with impeccable justice and courtesy. But a friend of mine who was having a supervision with him asked if he might consult him in his capacity as proctor, and swore that Greenway made him leave the room, knock and come in again. He was a deeply decent man, but massacres have resulted from his mind-set.

But I was not to learn. My education was a waste of time. I came out of Cambridge believing almost exactly, politically speaking, what I had believed in the Young Socialists at the age of sixteen, but with my views all the more entrenched by having seen the system at close quarters. Even today, after some forty years in one set of dreaming spires or another, without prospect of parole or remission for good conduct, I find myself treating a certain kind of upper-middle-class type with the nervous alertness of a zoo-keeper in charge of some apparently docile but secretly vicious beast.

My own early experience as a don was not of the happiest. I was elected at the age of twenty-one to a research fellowship at a rather stuffy, intellectually mediocre Cambridge college, full of rugger buggers, academic time-servers and upper-class louts, which seemed to put more store by how often one dined at High Table than how finely one might teach or write. My colleagues were accordingly faced with a dilemma when I came up for promotion to a full Fellowship, since though I had already published a book and acquired some reputation as a teacher, I preferred by and large to chew pieces of nutty slack and knock back cups of slime in my room rather than spend an evening amongst doddering, quasi-fascistic clergymen at High Table who talked of Gladstone's Irish Home Rule Bill as though it could still be headed off with a spot of ingenuity, and discussed various strategies for re-colonizing India. On one of the few evenings when I steeled myself to endure this dismal ceremony, I found to my dismay that the somewhat senile president of High Table, who was later to kill himelf out of sheer boredom, failed entirely to recognize me and mistook me for a kitchen boy who had arrived to inform them of some last-minute change of menu.

There was an additional complication. In an unpremeditated outburst of altruism, which I would later come to rue, I had become a driver for Meals on Wheels, and spent one morning a week ferrying a co-worker and a pile of malodorous ready-made lunches around the town. This made me an honorary woman, since the operation was run by the Women's Voluntary Service. My last contact with this outfit had been as a child, when they selected our family to be recipients of an American food parcel just after the war. We evidently qualified as part of the deserving poor, though as far as Americans go I have since occasionally bitten the hand that fed me. I have, however, married one as well, which is surely gratitude enough.

My co-volunteer in Meals on Wheels, a Lady Bountiful-type professor's wife, sized me up sexually on our first encounter before wisely deciding that I was too much of a geek to be worth fluttering an eyelid at. Neither of us had much sense of direction, and we sometimes arrived three or so hours later at the dingy apartment of some ravenous old-age pensioner, fearfully expecting to find his skeletal remains on the carpet as a result of our dilatoriness. It was often more a question of Late Suppers rather than Lunches on Wheels, as we wove our way unsteadily through labyrinthine housing estates in search of the elusive objects of our charity. A few of our customers were as malodorous as the meals, and my companion would hold a perfumed handkerchief to her nose as she tripped daintily to and fro with their minced meat, boiled carrots and rice pudding, trying not to gag.

Having been invited to write a guest column for *Granta*, the University's literary magazine, I decided to sketch a satirical contrast between the poor quality of Meals on Wheels and the outrageous self-indulgence of High Table. My own college spent far more each year on feeding its face than it did on the library. But the piece disastrously backfired. Though I had emphasized that my criticisms were in no sense of the admirable Meals on Wheels workers themselves, the whole organization took instant umbrage and cast me out as a toffee-nosed fifth columnist who had insinuated himself into their ranks in order to cast aspersions on their rice pudding. I was unmasked as the Kim Philby of Cambridge Meals on Wheels, and various of my elderly customers, biting the hand that fed them with the few teeth still left in their head, claimed with the wisdom of hindsight to have sensed my unsoundness. A torrent of letters from irate citizens were fired off to the *Cambridge Evening News*, inquiring just what right this grouse-swollen, sherry-soaked don had to sneer at the boiled carrots of the populace. Meanwhile, my college icily noted my assault on their dining habits just as they were agonizing over whether to re-elect me. I found myself trapped between town and gown, minced meat and *Magret à la d'Artagnan*, a traitor to both camps. In the end I was re-elected, but only, I suspect, because even the dodderers who wanted to have young Gladstone hanged for treason would have found it hard to acknowledge openly that they rated a man's consumption of walnuts over his contribution to scholarship.

The *Granta* episode was one example of the way that,

though shy and fatally un-self-confident, I was forever getting myself into the kind of scrapes which one would expect of a more boisterous, self-assertive character. I no more understood the logic of this than I understood how my pancreas worked. Perhaps it was genetic, since I had a cousin, a meek, rather pious soul, who suffered from much the same syndrome. He once woke up after a gargantuan drinking session to find himself lying in the empty compartment of a deserted train which seemed to be parked in some railway sidings in the middle of nowhere. Deep snow stretched to the horizon on every side, and he could spot no sign of life. He got down from the train and began to trudge through the snow, when he noticed a small fire or brazier burning in the distance, with a few dim figures gathered around it. As he drew nearer the brazier he could see that the figures were mostly old women dressed in black shawls, who were watching his approach impassively. Feeling something of a fool, he stumbled up and asked one of the women where he was, to which she replied 'Warsaw'. His last memory was of being in Liverpool. Could he somehow have been borne, unconscious, on to a ship? Then he realized that the old woman had replied to a question in English in English, and that she had in fact said 'Walsall'. It was the Midlands accent which had momentarily confused him. But to this day he has no idea how he got from Liverpool to Walsall.

Oxbridge dons, even non-bisexual ones, have always had it both ways. They are proud of their unworldly integrity, yet they also educate the rulers of tomorrow, thus enjoying some vicarious power while keeping their hands clean. The traditional don was an amphibious animal, moving between

Mayfair party and ivory tower rather like a monk untrue to his vows. They relished celebrity and the good life, while meditating in their studies on the vanity of human wishes and the eternal transience of things. Only the cloistered could be so pathetically star-struck by the worldly. Even today, they are prepared to throw their scholarly standards to the winds when it comes to appointing some averagely intelligent social networker with a media presence. But dons are also trustees of richly endowed charities known as colleges, and thus have a lot of clout of their own. Some of them would far rather be remembered as the bursar who ran up a new building than as the author of a ground-breaking study of Byzantium. And doing the one may always provide a convenient excuse for not getting round to the other.

These flamboyant, mythological figures are nowadays rare, glimpsed occasionally in some Oxford glade or found long-buried beneath some senior common-room armchair. Petulant, snobbish, spiteful, arrogant, autocratic and ferociously self-centred, they were a pretty squalid bunch. They were certainly not much of an advertisement for the benefits of education. As free as prima donnas from the dull constraints of reality, they had time to obstruct their colleagues' promotion, provide some charismatic chairmanship of the college tree committee, or even throw off a slim volume of Renaissance Latin verse. 'Boring' was their code-word for the lower classes, 'amusing' was their highest term of praise, and 'loyalty' meant lying and twisting in the interests of your cronies while ruthlessly worsting your enemies. They sported a distinctive Oxbridge combination of pedantry and frivolity, the latter providing some light relief from the former. Both vices are at one in their distaste for utility. They had soft, unused, pampered faces, like rural clergymen trying to behave with all the wicked brio of an Oscar Wilde.

A single word suffices to excuse these foibles: eccentricity. If a don spits in your beef stew or allows his pet parrot to lacerate your cheekbone, he is simply being lovably idiosyncratic. Many old-style academics have preferred to be thought colourful rather than honest. Their aim is to be fine, not good. Eccentricity, a fancy word for outrageous egoism, was to traditional Oxbridge what normality is to police sergeants. The homosexual John Sparrow opposed homosexual law reform on the grounds that it would take the spice out of being gay. A disgusting old misogynist who derived a positively erotic *frisson* from resisting enlightened reform, this malicious, supremely trivial-minded Warden of All Souls (or All Holes, as the college became known after he gleefully spotted a passage about buggery in D. H. Lawrence) had no interest in ideas, chalked up no academic or other achievements worth noting, and thought it amusing to joke about killing babies.

Another such erudite brat was the Cambridge historian Frederick Simpson, who I remember tottering every evening across Great Court for pre-High Table sherry with the Master of the college. He was said to be vile and humiliating to the college staff, and his contribution to the Second World War consisted in gathering honey, Pooh-Bear-like, in the countryside, which he then ate himself. Quite how this was meant to bring Hitler to his knees was unclear. His Cambridge counterpart George 'Dadie' Rylands, a member of the English Faculty, had about as much clue how to analyse literary works as a giraffe, but could read the stuff aloud quite beautifully, and received several honours for doing so.

Sex with this emotional desperado was said to be like being in a rugby scrum. Like several dons of his time, Rylands moved in a louche *beau monde* of upper-class loungers, fickle in friendship and volatile of temperament, but was judged by his friends to rank among the 'wisest, justest and best'.

There was also the President of Magdalen College, Oxford, who invited a freshman, an Indian prince, to sherry, and was told by the prince that his name in English meant 'Son of God'. 'Ah, yes,' replied the Master, 'we have the sons of a good many famous men in the college.' An Oxford colleague of his, a Fellow of Brasenose, had been an undergraduate tutor for many years and finally decided to give it up as a bad job. He did not wish to relinquish his Fellowship, however, so he asked the college to create a special post for him, in order to continue collecting his college stipend without the indignity of actually having to work. The college Fellows pooled their formidable intellectual resources and in the fullness of time came up with the post of President of Senior Common Room Dessert. The Fellow in question fulfilled these duties for many years with admirable conscientiousness, even constructing a complicated system of fines for Fellows who took dessert in the wrong order.

One of my own teachers at Cambridge, a retired public schoolmaster in a tweed suit and a walrus moustache, used occasionally to declaim poetry aloud *à la* Rylands, since he had nothing intelligent to say about it. Having nothing to say about it, he just said it instead. At the end of a prolonged, deafening bout of declamation, he would sit back, clutch his belly and announce complacently: 'It's all a matter of the stomach muscles, you know.' Studying English literature seemed largely a matter of the stomach muscles. Someone had obviously made the mistake of telling this entirely harmless old codger that he was a bit of a rogue, so that he would chortlingly report to us some extraordinarily mild risqué comment he had made to someone else, perhaps thirty years ago. He would then thrust his tongue literally into his cheek and raise his eyebrows, mutely inviting us to burst out with cries of 'You wicked old devil!' or 'God, you're a caution!'

Oxbridge is a great breeder of young fogeys. For every don there is a mini-don, a prematurely stooped twenty-odd-year-old with a pipe, a crimson waistcoat, an outsized cranium and a shrivelled heart, who wears his pedantry like a regimental tie. One such precociously decrepit character was an undergraduate of mine called Gulliver, who if he had not had the good fortune to be prematurely bald would no doubt have torn away great tufts of his hair until he had come to resemble the senior dons he most revered. These certainly did not include myself. He was one of the few Platonists I have ever encountered, and believed in Plato's doctrine of the Forms rather as other people believe in proportional representation or the beneficial effects of carrot juice. He would arrive at our tutorials on hot summer days wearing a heavy three-piece tweed suit like a man clamped in a coffin. He could easily have combed his hair by looking into his shoes, and wore a shirt collar sharp enough to draw blood. He was also the only undergraduate of mine who ever wore a gown, if one sets aside a charming yellow-locked hippie, now a BBC television producer, who wore a gown but rather spoiled the effect by wearing no shoes or socks with it.

The first ten minutes or so of Gulliver's tutorial would be taken up with his ritual unrobing. Whatever the weather, he would hook a large furled umbrella gingerly to the back of

his seat, before proceeding to divest himself daintily of a
sleek pair of kid gloves. These he would lay with priestly
precision on the table between us, after which he would
produce a minute, opulent-looking leather-bound notebook
and a gleaming fountain pen. I had sometimes thought of
poisoning the glass of sherry I gave him, dumping his body
down some ravine and nicking his fountain pen. His hand-
writing was that of an anally retentive mouse. All of this
preliminary activity would be accompanied by a subcurrent
of discreet smiles and self-deprecating moues between us, as
I would find myself gesturing him to his chair, nodding
tenderly at his gloves, and generally behaving like a barber
pathetically desperate for custom. His effect on me was
strangely paralytic, and I could hear a hoarse, strangulated
tone creep into my voice as I invited him to unburden upon
me the fruits of his week's work. There were times when I
would far rather have had a hippo unburden his bowels all
over me, but duty was duty.

Gulliver would then remove his essay from his briefcase
with a single clinical gesture, and announce its title in a
languid tone. He might open his mouth and say something
like 'Some Unlikenesses between Two Novels by Miss
Austen', or 'Some Uses of the Term "Kindness" in a Short
Story by Mr Forster'. He was always scrupulously polite in
his allusions to authors, and it seemed uncharacteristically
insolent of him not to refer to Mr Sophocles. He would then
read out his thoughts on these recklessly avant-garde topics
in a parsonical sing-song, occasionally taking up his mag-
nificent fountain pen to make some microscopic correction
to his text. He read his essays in a robotic, dissociated sort
of way, as though he had never seen them before, or was

translating from the Sanskrit as he went along. They were elegant, empty productions, as impossible to criticize as a bowl of goldfish.

There was one occasion, however, on which Gulliver committed a grotesque, utterly inexplicable blunder. Having been asked for the title of his essay, he replied, 'Some Aspects of Colour Imagery in "The Ancient Mariner" by William Wordsworth.' This was as stunning an error as if he had removed his trousers rather than his gloves, and I ought of course to have instantly intervened to correct it. As in some strange out-of-body experience, however, I saw myself sitting paralysed and powerless in my armchair as he began to churn out his blandly symmetrical sentences. Two whole paragraphs had now unfurled, the moment for intervention had vanished for ever. I had cravenly chickened out, and I now had nothing to contemplate but the vision of how, in some ten minutes' time, I would have to break to him the appalling news that the author of 'The Ancient Mariner' was Coleridge.

The essay was actually rather better than usual. It demonstrated some plausible connections between 'The Ancient Mariner' and the rest of Wordsworth's poetry, and for one crazed moment I wondered whether Gulliver had just made the literary find of the century. But the moment of truth had now arrived, and in my best bedside manner I let him know, without rushing dogmatically to endorse the view, of the general scholarly consensus concerning the poem's authorship. On the whole he took this revelation rather well. A dull flush spread slowly up from his razor-like collar to his receding hairline, but rather than rush out in search of a convenient abyss to hurl himself down he gave a small, rueful smile. At one of our last meetings, shortly before he graduated, I asked him what sort of career he intended to pursue, and he replied that intended eventually to become an Anglican priest. He added, however, that he felt the need for some experience of the world before doing so, and was therefore looking for a post in the Bodleian Library.

For all their horrors, the dons were an egregiously witty bunch. Sir Maurice Bowra, of whom John Sparrow remarked that his prose was unreadable and his verse unprintable, dubbed the gay leftist Oxbridge of his day the Homintern, and observed of the gaudily dressed French scholar Enid Starkie that she had appeared at one of his parties 'in all the colours of the Rimbaud'. 'Heard of any amusing deaths recently?' the ageing Bowra was wont to inquire. 'Buggers can't be choosers,' he remarked when announcing his engagement to a rather plain woman. Brow-beating and grotesquely partisan, with a voracious craving for public honours, Bowra was nonetheless a genuine liberal of the old school, a champion of justice and liberty.

He was certainly a champion of me. Years ago, he inter-viewed me for a Fellowship at his college, along with Lord David Cecil. The two men were both on the point of retire-ment, and both fairly deaf. They seemed to be able to hear neither myself nor each other, but appeared not a whit abashed by this deficiency and rattled merrily on. Most of the authors I mentioned in the course of the interview seemed to have been personal friends of theirs, or in Bowra's case sometimes partners in sodomy, so that their interjec-tions consisted largely of cries of 'Ah, dear old Evelyn!', 'Poor dear Virginia!', 'How absolutely typical of Wystan!' and the like. When I mentioned Chaucer, I half-expected them to shout in unison 'Good old Geoffrey!'

After a while Bowra grew bored with the interview and asked me whether I had seen his copper beech tree. I was unsure whether this was some sort of homosexual code, but he leapt to his feet, leaving Cecil dozing benignly in his armchair, and marched me out into the college garden, which contained the largest copper beech tree in England. We stood silently shoulder to shoulder in front of the tree as the dusk gathered, and I must have made some appropriately witty or poetic comment on the tree, since I got the job. I think Cecil had taken a shine to me, as the landowner harbours a secret sympathy for the poacher. Sullen prole and carefree patrician linked hands over the heads of the conformist middle classes. I won my Fellowship largely because of the romanticism of one member of the upper classes and the erotic interest of another.

Academic life in the United States, where erotic interest is something you can take courses in, is a different affair. I was once invited by a Mormon university in Utah to come and teach them about ideology. Teaching Mormons about ideology is something of a coals-to-Newcastle operation, rather like instructing the Spice Girls in public relations or encouraging Mike Tyson to work up a bit of aggression. These, after all, are the people who believe that when they die they, or at least the menfolk, will each rule over his own custom-made universe like God or Bill Gates, with their wives at their elbows as a kind of Mrs God. Their religion is for the most part a scandalized reaction to the fact that Jesus had the poor taste not to get himself born into white middle-class America, but for some unfathomable reason chose instead to pitch in with a lot of scruffy, unhygienic Jews in the days before four-star hotels were invented.

Black Americans were admitted to their priesthood somewhat late in the day, homosexuals were submitted to some questionable forms of treatment, and their attitude towards women is not quite that of Andrea Dworkin. Nowadays, like Ulster Unionists, their more canny spokespeople present them as a victimized postmodern minority. Just as some Ulster Unionists, having picked up the language of the cultural studies departments, have the cheek these days to define their Britishness as a commitment to a multi-ethnic society, so a few Mormons are no doubt now spouting on about 'marital pluralism' or 'flexible multi-choice gender affiliations' when they mean polygamy. Male members of this university, including the teaching staff, were not allowed to wear beards unless they were infected with some loathsome disease of the jaw, and even then they had to carry a 'beard card' testifying to the fact. They seemed to have only a dim idea of who I was, and if they had had a clearer one would probably not have invited me in the first place. But since their previous guest had been Lord Dacre (Hugh Trevor-Roper), it is possible that they could not tell one Englishman from another.

They proved, however, to be a genial enough bunch, and after each of my lectures flocked eagerly to join me over lunch. I learned later that this was because they were being paid to do so. It was admittedly rather awkward to have to be driven more or less into the middle of the desert whenever I wanted a cup of coffee, and cigarettes, to which I was then devoted, were an even more troublesome matter. Since there was nowhere on the campus where I could smoke, least of all the open air, I took to crouching like a guilty schoolboy in the lavatory cubicle, and on one such occasion heard two

Mormons enter the room and start to sniff. 'Hey, Hal,' one said to the other, six inches from my shouder, 'it smells just like somebody's been smoking in here!' But he said it in a jovial, joshing sort of tone, eliciting no more than a polite chuckle from his companion, since he could not of course seriously imagine that someone actually had, indeed at that very moment actually was. The idea that a cigarette had been lit in the place was as inconceivable as the president of the university cavorting around the campus in false boobs and fish-net stockings.

After a while, I began to feel like a character in one of those science fiction stories where people around you appear perfectly normal until suddenly, by some stray word or gesture, they betray the fact that they are aliens. Every time I stumbled upon someone who appeared to be moderately human, he would end up saying something like, 'You know, I think *Middlemarch* is kind of a Mormon text,' which would resonate in my mind with the dissonant chords of a horror movie. Affable young men who would chat sensibly to me about socialism or Shakespeare would leave casually behind on their chairs a copy of the Book of Mormon, with a marker against some piece of portentous gobbledygook and a coy note reading: 'Terry, this is a challenge from me to you.' I had only two friends to consult over these mysteries, one a closet human being who still scrupulously maintained the outward appearance of an alien since his parents were big shots in the church, and the other a young woman whom I have since married. When I asked what this note meant, they told me that it meant that if I didn't see the point of the passage immediately, I was damned to hell. Hell would have been a welcome respite from Provo, Utah.

As a languisher in the outer darkness, I was not admitted to the holier bits of the Salt Lake City temple; but I was allowed into the profane outer precincts, where I was invited to watch a film called 'The Meaning of Life'. I had always thought that this was a Monty Python movie, but it turned out to be a surreally brief summary of the meaning of life, a meaning which has now completely slipped my mind, delivered to camera by a group of manically grinning Mormons with families so enormous they made the Irish look positively sterile. My two faithful friends, flanking me in the cinema, whispered various bits of helpful information into my ear: this woman with the baby on her knee, talking of how the Holy Spirit could augment your bank account, was a suicidal alcoholic, while the man sporting the bible and the big hair was a wife-beater, indeed a multiple-wife beater.

It was their lethal American blandness which proved hardest to take. If I spoke to them of the evils of patriarchy, they were all nods and smiles; if I suggested that the Mormon Church, with its doglike devotion to the wealthy and powerful, was a grotesque travesty of the Christian gospel, they fell over themselves to concur. The only thing they really couldn't take was smoking. After I left, a heated controversy over my visit broke out in the pages of the campus newspaper, but it seemed to revolve more around Marlboro than Marxism. I had, however, had my glimpse of Temple garments, which was enough in itself to make my trip worthwhile. Temple garments are a special kind of underwear worn by Mormon men, and by peeking up the shorts of a young man sprawled sunbathing on the grass, I joined that select group of the damned who have actually laid eyes on them. The idea is that when Jesus comes again, his divine effulgence will

burn the pants off people; but these particular knickerbock-
ers, being woven of a sort of spiritual asbestos, will stay firmly
in place, indeed will light up so that the Lord may recognize
his own. Only Mormon men who have completed their stint
on the missions – which is to say, those glazed, dark-suited
young zombies whose task is to doorstep the damned for a
couple of years and try to stay out of bed with each other –
have the privilege of wearing these panties, and no self-
respecting young Mormon woman would go on a date with
a man who did not. Some Mormon men who have not yet
won their knickers have been known to wear an elastic band
under their trousers when going on a date, to create a
phantom panty-line.

Not all of my visits to the States have been so disagreeable.
I was once asked to speak at a mid-west college to an undergraduate class which was bravely ploughing its way through
the lengthiest of all English novels, Samuel Richardson's
eighteenth-century masterpiece *Clarissa*. It was towards the
end of the semester, the class was flagging a little, and the
professor running it thought that, since I had just published
a study of Richardson, it might prove a diversion to have me
in. I chatted for a while about my book on *Clarissa*, and
noticed that this provoked a few rustles and nudges on the
back rows. It began to dawn on me that some of the less
intellectually athletic of the company thought that I *was*
Samuel Richardson. I was, after all, an Englishman talking
about my book with 'Clarissa' in the title, I must have looked
pretty old to them, and their grasp of history was perhaps
less than perfect.

They did not, however, noisily demand to know why I
was responsible for having them stagger through such an

inordinately long piece of fiction, since American students are invariably courteous. So, indeed, are Chinese students, though they are also a good deal shyer. On one of my trips to Beijing, where I was ceremonially presented on arrival with a set of pirated translations of my own works, the students, being too bashful to ask questions in public after my lectures, wrote them instead on little scraps of paper and passed them up to me. I ended up with a deskful of inquiries to choose from, the first one of which I opened read: 'Which is the greater writer, George Eliot or Agatha Christie?' Like a crook running a raffle, I palmed it hastily and selected another. Teaching in China in the mid-80s, it was hard to know what they knew of Western culture and what they didn't. The word 'Freud' might elicit a blank, but someone would ask me how the Liverpool poets were getting on. My partner at the time gave a lecture on feminism and was asked by a young Chinese woman to explain what pornography was. This particular piece of despicable ignorance, I imagine, has now been efficiently put to rights.

7

Aristos

Not all of my encounters with the English upper classes have proved as amiable as my interview with Bowra and Cecil. My experience with the Queen, for example, has not been without its difficulties. I was strolling in Oxford one day when I noticed a small clutch of people on the other side of the street, eagerly craning their necks towards a bend in the road. At that moment, a fleet of black limousines and a few pairs of police outriders swept into sight, the last of the limos bearing Her Majesty. She had, I think, been unveiling a plaque somewhere. Her loyal subjects across the way waved and cheered, and the Queen turned in her seat to acknowledge their greeting. Then, in a Pavlovian reflex, and with the sublime impartiality one would expect of a monarch, she turned graciously to my side of the street as well. Unfortunately I was the only person on that pavement, and it was more than my political reputation was worth to stop and blow her a kiss. So I cut her dead and strolled defiantly on, expecting at any moment a heavy hand to fall on my shoulder and to find myself led away in shackles to the Tower of London. Perhaps because he had got wind of this insult to his mother, or more likely because he disapproves of academics who hold that it's all right to drop your aitches, Prince Charles once remarked to some Oxford Rhodes Scholars that he hoped they were not taught by 'that dreadful Terry Eagleton'.

My next major encounter with the aristocracy took place in more sombre circumstances. One of my brightest undergraduates, an ex-Etonian called Justin, hailed from a troubled background which led him eventually to take his own life just before his final exams. He was the son of a European countess and the nephew of a Scottish lord, and a youth of such pedigree would not usually have chosen to read English at Oxford, certainly not with a notoriously left-wing Tutor at a socially undistinguished college with a name like a department store. But Justin had the resolution and independence of his breed, as well as the keen social conscience of the more liberal-minded aristocrat; and he was in the painful process of transforming himself into a socialist when his early death overtook him.

I was sent by the college as its representative to his funeral in the Scottish Lowlands, and was picked up at Edinburgh airport by a stout, bustling little woman who shook my hand with the grip of a stevedore and announced that she was dotty. I realized after a moment that this probably meant Dotty, and she then introduced me to her titled husband Hoppy, a middle-aged man so absurdly tall that he sagged in the middle like a soggy chip. Hoppy was so dim that he could hardly talk, but on the rare occasion that he managed to rise to the challenge of verbal articulation, he spoke with all the crispness and dryness of *Muscadet sur lie*. At one point he got out of the car to relieve himself copiously by the roadside, exposing his member with cavalier unconcern to the gaze of the passing plebs. It took him so long to clamber out of the car that I began to wonder whether 'Hoppy' was meant to be ironic.

Lady Dotty drove us through the Lowlands like a thing possessed, blinking myopically through the windscreen and overtaking at high speed on lip-bitingly narrow bends. When she was forced to slow down by some contemptibly law-abiding vehicle which was observing the speed limit, she would turn to Hoppy in the passenger seat, curl her lip and spit the words 'Huh! Careful driver!' at him like an expletive. Hoppy would nod gravely, his back bolt upright, his head only a centimetre or so from the car roof. It occurred to me that we might be *en route* to more funerals than one. There was little conversation, but at one point as I was lolling, faintly nauseous from Dotty's maniacal driving, in the back seat, she suddenly barked to me, 'Do you know Lord Crichton?' I replied that I did not, at which she snapped, 'He's behind you,' like a pantomime dame. I wondered for a moment whether there was a member of the nobility crouching behind the back seat of the car, or perhaps lurking in the boot, when I realized that she meant behind me on the road. I turned and saw through the rear window a thick-set, prognathous young man with quivering, blood-hound-like jowls in the driving seat of the car following us. He saw me looking and gave me an ambiguous gesture, either of greeting or derision.

We arrived at last in the small Scottish village which bore Justin's family title. Skirting the big house, which was boarded up to save ruinous expense, we halted at a terraced row of farm labourers' cottages on the estate, which had been knocked together to form an alternative family home.

A policeman at the gates drew himself to attention and saluted as we passed. Either he had recognized Lady Dotty or he was a fan of literary theory. Half of the Scottish aristocracy seemed to have crammed themselves into the labourers' cottages. The furniture had fallen on hard times, though the whisky was plentiful. I noticed how shabbily dressed the guests were, the frowsy, willowy women kitted out in defiantly dowdy skirts and blouses, with perhaps a black scarf thrown negligently over their shoulders in token honour of the occasion. Their large-handed, stammering menfolk, all looking vaguely alike with recessive chins and elongated faces, lounged about in clothes which suggested they had just wandered in from planting turnips or unblocking the drains. In my hired black suit with tightly-buttoned waistcoat, I was by far the best-dressed member of the funeral, the conformist petty-bourgeois among the cavalier gentry. Those who dictate the forms can afford to dispense with them. Most of the people there had the niceness of those whose wealth and status allow them to live without arrogance.

On the basis of our brief exchange of glances on the road, I fell into stilted conversation with young Lord Crichton, who looked only about twenty-two. I asked him had he studied at Oxford or Cambridge, knowing this to be a tribal custom of his ilk, and after a lengthy pause, during which he thoroughly digested the question, he replied slowly that he had not, a fact which his difficulty with a simple question had already more or less confirmed. He spoke his few words like a man trying out some fiendishly difficult language which he had picked up a smattering of but had not yet dared to practise in public. He then stared out of the window at the

Lowlands for a long time, to indicate that he had nothing particular to say to me but did not consider himself sufficiently bound by the social forms to conceal this fact by indulging in pointless small talk.

It was clear that he expected me to understand this and not be tediously suburban enough to take offence at it, and the fact that despite his silence he bore me no ill will soon became apparent. I had been fidgeting for some time in my jacket pocket, toying with a cigarette packet which I was longing to raid, being at the time a smoker, but which convention obviously forbade. I was sure that my fidgeting had been only mild and furtive, but I suddenly found myself staring at a cigarette which Lord Crichton had produced in a single skilled sweep from his pocket like a pistol, and was holding silently out to me. We lit up together without a word, in a moment of mutual need which like Catherine and Heathcliff cut clean through the class system. Nobody around us objected; indeed I had the feeling that they would not have objected if it had been something rather more sensational than a cigarette that he was thrusting towards me.

I was introduced next to a burly, dwarfish man of advanced years, his complexion a vivid puce from many decades of riotous living. He invited me to call him Mickey, though this was not in fact his name, and I later discovered that he owned a large slice of Aberdeenshire. Once again, as an opening conversational gambit, I asked him if he had been at Oxford, and he responded that he had been at the House, a rather old-fashioned way of referring to Christ Church. I inquired what subject he had studied there, only to find that this innocent question plunged him into as much bemusement as if I had asked him to list the various dialects of Tanzania or the geological peculiarities of Brandenburg. After some non-committal shuffling and muttering, he answered rather cagily that he had studied law, but I had the impression that this was something of a guess. He then spoke a little about his life in the House of Lords, before switching abruptly to a discussion of my surname. 'Scottish name, isn't it?' he asked, and I agreed that it was. 'I know that, you see, my boy,' he went on, 'because one of my dearest pals is called Eagleton.' Since he had just been talking about the Lords, I asked if he meant someone there. 'Good God, no,' he replied, 'he's my ghillie.' Somewhere in Aberdeenshire there is a gamekeeper who may look a little like myself. Gamekeepers and gatekeepers are not perhaps so different.

Mickey then produced the most dramatic conversation-stopper I have ever heard. Glancing around at the funeral guests, he declared loudly: 'Funny thing, suicide. My wife and daughter died by their own hand.' He delivered this information in the equable tones of one remarking on a slight change in the weather, before going on to speak of something quite different. I have sometimes wondered since what an appropriate response might have been. 'What, both at the same time?' would be an obvious inquiry, though if he had been less genial I might have risked 'Are you surprised?' But by now he was telling me that one of his sons was standing for parliament. I checked myself just in time from asking for which political party.

After a while, I realized that the men were as ludicrously tall as they were because most of them either were or had been officers in the Scots Guards. Indeed, almost everyone in the place, including the women, exuded some sort of military aroma. A Scottish piper droned away mournfully by the graveside, and the towering clergyman, clearly another Scots Guard in disguise, preached a sermon in which he described Justin's brief, agonized life as the equivalent of what the army calls a 'hard posting'. After serving out his commission on earth, the boy had now returned to heavenly base. Afterwards, driving back in the car to Edinburgh airport with Dotty and Hoppy, Hoppy asked me what I thought of the sermon, and seemed rather distressed to learn that I thought it was a load of crap. Why, I asked irately from the back seat, fortified now by a few stiff glasses of Glenmorangie, did they have to see everything in terms of the army? 'Only a way of speaking, old boy,' murmured Hoppy, evidently something of a specialist in the philosophy of metaphor. I thought of asking him whether in that case it would be all right to put everything in terms of the revolutionary overthrow of the aristocracy, but instead watched the Scottish landscape flash by at terrifying speed and wondered what Justin would have made of his own interment. Hoppy and Dotty adroitly managed to shake me off at the airport, even though we were all travelling on the same flight to London. They had had what was probably the first encounter of their lives with a non-Conservative, and having discharged their duties towards me in *noblesse oblige* fashion had no intention of prolonging the agony by sitting beside me on the plane.

Someone I know who had met Justin when he was a small child predicted at the time that he would kill himself; and though I am rather sceptical of this prognostication, as well as of the *Brideshead* stereotype of the doomed aristocrat, there did seem a dark air of self-destructiveness about him, complexly entwined with an intense moral and intellectual passion. The aristocracy are a kind of pointless class, as gloriously useless as a work of art; and for the likes of Justin they thus had a secret affinity with the dispossessed. The displaced and the dispossessed could link hands behind the backs of the braying stockbrokers and hot-faced philistines. It was the old pact between landlord and poacher, one scandalous to the Eagletons or gamekeepers of this world. Those who have so much that they don't need to think about it can be as spendthrift as those who have nothing to lose.

The death drive has this kind of excessiveness about it, as is clear from that phoney English dandy, Oscar Wilde. Throughout Wilde's rake's progress in high society one can feel just this sickening sense of precariousness, this gathering hubris of a man who is riding too high, too brilliantly, and seems at times to be almost deliberately courting disaster. Just as his own profligate, irresponsible Anglo-Irish class back home finally pulled the roof down on their own heads, in an exuberant paroxysm of guilt and self-odium, so Wilde's outrageous flouting of conventional morality seems a race towards self-destruction, as though he was tempting English society to do their worst. And of course they, like him, found themselves able to resist everything but temptation.

This drive to self-undoing is often marked in the insider/ outsider – in those (non-)Patrons who, like Wilde, become too flawless a parody of the real thing to be entirely plausible. Wilde knew himself to be a fake, a sham, a man wearing a mask; so he would wreak his colonial vengeance by showing that all identity was a matter of pose and persona, all social forms passing and provisional. The colonial does not know who he is, while the gentleman does not care. If Wilde was superficial, he was profoundly so, and the closest he came to the truth was an ironic awareness of his own inauthenticity. The sexually, socially, ethnically doubled outsider from Doublin (as James Joyce spelt the city's name), who could never name himself with any assurance, would become a kind of fifth columnist in the enemy camp, unmasking their own complacent imperial selfhood for the fiction that it was, mocking as well as flattering their social and artistic forms by deploying them even more dexterously than they did themselves. Meanwhile, however, his portrait was festering away in a silent attic, and reality, for which Wilde had as fine a disdain as he had for last season's cut of waistcoat, was finally to feel his collar with heavy fingers and lead him off to hard labour. It was a rough fate for a man whose only previous physical exertion, as he observed, had been a spot of dominoes outside French cafés, and whose only previous experience of roughness had been with rent boys. Like many an outsider he had overstepped the mark, failed to appreciate that the Irishman's role was one of licensed jester to the English court, not a dangerous distraction from its rulers' business of breeding. To adopt the words of the Dublin wit Sean Mac Reamoinn, he ended up like the Irish census, broken down by age, sex and religion.

Perhaps it is not surprising that I should have found myself writing so often about this English-Irish Oxfordian proto-post-structuralist socialist, with his strange blending of patrician and Paddy, his Celtic combination of levity and seriousness. He fled a stagnant colony in time-honoured Irish fashion with only his linguistic wits to hawk, as I, like so many others, had nothing but linguistic capital to lever myself out of the working class. Language costs nothing, and as far as words go there's always more where that came from. But Wilde also interests me in his almost pathological aversion to platitude, another mark of the colonial. If he was homosexual, it was partly because heterosexuality seemed so intolerably clichéd. He had only to spot a norm to feel the almost intolerable urge to transgress it, and it is here, not in cheap hotel rooms, that his true perversity lies.

My first contact with Wilde's Anglo-Irish kind came on my first lecturing trip to Ireland in the early 60s. I was invited to speak in a debate by a Trinity College student society of impressive antiquity, and arrived at the airport to find myself met by a stout, florid-faced young Irishman called Nigel. Nobody in Ireland is called Nigel. He was wearing curious patches of white material over his shoes, which turned out to be spats. I had read about spats in Victorian novels, but had assumed that they went out with bustles and penny-farthing bicycles. (In similar vein, Raymond Williams once told me that F. R. Leavis had jogged past him in Cambridge one morning in the pouring rain, then trotted back about twenty minutes later with typical courtesy, drenched to the bone, to apologize for having 'cut' him. Williams had previously only come across the word in public-school stories.) Nigel, however, turned out to be an amiable fellow, and introduced me to his fellow committee members, who had names like Julian and Mark. Hardly anyone in Ireland is called Julian or Mark. These were young Anglo-Irish gents, for whom Trinity College was an Oxbridge-by-the-Liffey. The debate was conducted in evening dress, and there were a number of respectful allusions to the 'distinguished essayist', whom I took to be some venerable, long-deceased member of the society but who turned out to be myself.

*

The Wildean epigram takes an English platitude and rips it apart, turns it inside out, stands it on its head. Like the epigram, the colonial subject is a kind of deviance, a piece of the metropolis bungled, travestied, gone suddenly awry; but something of the same is true of the aristocratic wit, and in Wilde the two are intimately coupled. Eccentricity is the nobility's equivalent of colonial perversity. The upper classes are so luxuriantly free that they are absolved from conforming to their own customs, let alone anybody else's. Their conduct is not to be restricted by anything as drearily two-a-penny as reality. As an apprentice Oxford don, I once found myself sitting beside a colleague with a somewhat harassed air at a college meeting, and just to make conversation asked him how many children he had. A faint chill settled on the surrounding company, as they realized that I had committed the frightful solecism of forcing a colleague into a prosaic observation. It is hard to reply to such a question while simultaneously marking one's difference from solicitors' clerks and cinema attendants. But my colleague was not to be coerced. 'Oh, thousands and thousands', he responded airily. At home, cleaning up the soggy cornflakes, he was compelled to be a Roundhead; here at least he could be a Cavalier. Home was for the good, college for the fine. The philosopher Gilbert Ryle, who pointed out that 'to make a mental note' means not to make a note at all, was once asked by a colleague at High Table when he could hope to see his next book. 'You can hope whenever you like,' Ryle replied.

Sociology, the study of what is common, recurrent and predictable in human life, is essentially the study of clichés. It thus comes as no surprise that the upper classes are implacably opposed to the discipline. It is the middle class's riposte to upper-class eccentricity. The fact that the queues at supermarket checkout points will all be roughly the same length is a matter of sociology. To say 'I love you' is pure sociology, however sincerely one may mean it. For the Romantics, it is tragic that we are forced to express our most uniquely individual feelings in phrases shop-soiled by millions of others; for the modernist, it is only by the use of such phrases that we can express our feelings to ourselves. I once heard a sociologist recount how he had walked into his university department to find his secretary in tears. Having consoled her as best he could, he strolled down the corridor and glanced into another office, only to see another secretary in tears. 'One secretary in tears', he remarked, 'is tragedy. Two is sociology.' Dr Greenway, as we shall see in a moment, would no doubt have agreed, though it is not clear why two weeping secretaries does not double the tragedy rather than dilute it.

Clichés have their historical fashions, like the rest of our discourse. The American satirist Tom Lehrer, who declared that he abandoned satire altogether when Henry Kissinger was awarded the Nobel Peace Prize, remarked that when he was a student there were certain things that you could not say in front of a girl. Now, he added, you can say anything you like except 'girl'. English politicians used to say things like 'I have never courted popularity', but their most recurrent phrase these days is 'very clear', since they know that they are suspected of being slippery.

A friend of mine once wondered whether there was a clause in the contract of Hollywood scriptwriters requiring them to insert the phrase 'Try to get some sleep' in every screenplay they wrote. It is a remarkably frequent piece of advice in movies, less legendary than 'The men are getting restless' or 'It's quiet . . . too quiet', but more common these days than the screen clichés I remember from childhood, such as 'You're hurting my arm' and 'Go to your room', the latter addressed by a parent to an errant child. Changing familial structures have rendered this order obsolete, since these days that is where they are likely to be in the first place, sullenly cold-shouldering their kinsfolk. The venerable 'Just touch the bell if you need anything' has also been a casualty of social change, though 'This isn't the way to the airport!', spoken in an anxious yelp from the back seat of a taxi and followed by a close-up of a shifty-looking driver, has simply died of fatigue.

There used to be whole slices of dialogue which cropped up on both large and small screens with striking frequency, such as 'Take a seat' . . . 'Thank you, I prefer to stand' . . . 'As you wish', or 'But that's blackmail!' . . . 'Let's just call it a business arrangement.' Most Westerns statutorily included the following metaphysical exchange: 'You've got to stop running. What are you running from anyway?' . . . 'I dunno. Maybe – myself.' These have now mostly perished, but other screen stereotypes are more stubborn. In English police stations on screen, anyone above the rank of sergeant is invariably in a chronic state of *Weltschmertz*, archly jocose with their peers and wearily sarcastic with their underlings. Sardonic banter is the currency of all fictional cop-shops. Senior boffins in the British intelligence services are still easy to spot: when you enter their office they are always engaged in some amiably eccentric pastime like feeding mice to a boa constrictor, and will murmur without looking up 'Funny things, reptiles . . .' in response to your heated announcement that the Chinese have just invaded Finland.

Arrested spies, murderers and assorted maniacs will always be described to police officers by their neighbours as living quietly and keeping themselves to themselves, while psychopaths still tend to speak in robotic, softly sinister tones. They no longer necessarily have a crazed look about them, however, since the latest platitude is that paedophiles and serial killers look just like you and me, buy postage stamps and say things like 'Looks like rain.' Screen criminals, on the other hand, are still often jittery, foul-mouthed creatures with permanently frayed nerves, unable to lift a coffee cup without an impatience which betrays their moral degeneracy. Complex criminal operations which demand some delicate coordination – digging a tunnel under the Bank of England, for example – are conducted on screen by men in a state of psychotic irritability with each other, rather than, as surely must be the case in real life, with the quietly correct efficiency of undertakers. When suspects are interviewed by the police, the scriptwriters' union insists that the following piece of dialogue ensues: 'Just a minute, why are you asking me all these questions?' 'It's just routine' . . . 'But you've asked me all this already' . . . 'Let's just go through it one more time, OK?'

It is now only in old-fashioned thrillers that the character finally unmasked as the murderer says, 'Is this meant to be some sort of joke?' or 'You must be out of your mind!' But screen characters who have just been informed that their husband, lover or bosom pal is a spy, rapist or strangler still exclaim: 'But that's impossible! I mean, he'd never do a thing like that. I know him . . .' Since everybody knows somebody, this would exculpate the entire population. Real-life bank robbers, however, have almost certainly stopped shouting 'All right, everybody down on the floor! Just do what we say and you won't get hurt,' to save themselves grave social embarrassment. Apprehended villains who still say 'It's a fair cop' or 'You've got the wrong man' are postmodern ironists.

People in screen dramas in the grip of some powerful emotion are incapable of common sense, in a spurious equation of strong feeling with irrationality. 'Look, Inspector, my daughter is missing and all you can talk about is organizing a bloody search party.' Distraught victims tend to regard identification parades or house-to-house inquiries as monstrously cold-hearted pieces of bureaucracy. Detectives interviewing suspects still tend to stroll to the door, turn with their hand on the doorknob and murmur 'Oh, by the way, just one more thing,' before unleashing some devastating question.

Telephones on screen remain a serious source of unreality. Characters who pick up phones always hesitate a fraction longer than one would in real life before saying hello, while phones are allowed to ring nerve-rackingly longer than they would in the average bored or inquisitive household. Illogically, however, a rung number always replies instantly, even if it is British Rail Information. Swathes of complex information are absorbed down the phone with astounding rapidity, to forestall audience boredom. When a caller hangs up on you after an angry exchange, you must always stare at the receiver before replacing it, just as in pre-technological days you had to pump the receiver up and down shouting 'hello, hello!' when you were cut off, as though this would magically restore contact.

Clichés may be stale truths, but they are usually truths even so; and they contribute to our liberty by making social life predictable, automating parts of it so that we are free to attend to others. They are quotations without a source: nobody thinks of asking who first said 'There are some things more precious to me than money, you know,' or 'Unhand her, you dastardly brute!' But the clichés of yesterday may become the truths of tomorrow, just as it is now the last word in postmodernism to sit with your mates in a theatre dressed as a milkmaid or a German soldier and sing along to *The Sound of Music*. The catchword of the new police detective will be 'It's just routine', audiences will thrill to the demented shriek of 'There is no escape from this camp!', and it will be cool once more for villains to shout 'One false move and I'll fill you full of lead.'

My Cambridge supervisor Dr Greenway was an absurd figure, but no fool. In a typically conservative way he did not value human beings highly, and by and large preferred works of art and herbaceous borders to human beings; but he was unfailingly courteous and considerate, even when we threw up our mulled claret over his pixie-like feet at his parties, and even to a stroppy young rebel like myself. In my first year as an undergraduate he called me 'Eagleton', in my second year 'Terence', and in my third year 'Terry'. Perhaps if I had stayed on at his college beyond my undergraduate years, this escalating intimacy would have reached its natural conclusion in 'sweetiepie'. We spent much of our time discussing Marx or Lenin when we should have been talking about Wordsworth or Sophocles, and he turned out to know an impressive amount about these men, as he knew an impressive amount about everything. He did not of course agree with them, but neither did he bother disagreeing with them, since that would have been to betray an ungentlemanly partisanship. His social world was so serenely secure that he felt not the slightest need to refute socialist doctrine, a move which would have credited it with more reality than it deserved. There was no more point in refuting socialists than in refuting sceptics.

Indeed, I had the impression that at some deep level he did not really believe that any rational being could entertain such views; he treated me when I spoke of such matters as though I was advancing some zany hypothesis, flying a kite. Years later, when I was an academic, I was selling a socialist newspaper on an Oxford street when a colleague from the English Faculty passed by and looked straight at me. He saw that it was me, but he could not acknowledge the fact to himself. Assumption moved in quickly to blot out perception. It was as though he had spotted me in police uniform directing the traffic, or as if I had appeared at his restaurant table as a waiter. It is true that selling things on the street is the best way to guarantee your invisibility. If you want to be utterly anonymous in public, the surest way is to dress as a clown and dance up and down the pavement with a bundle of leaflets under your arm. But I am certain that my colleague saw me and then didn't, as Othello does and does not believe that Desdemona is a whore. Seeing is disbelieving.

Despite his disbelief, Greenway was quite willing to discuss socialism, as one might discuss the ventilation system of ancient Sparta or the average body-weight of a four-year-old warthog. All of these subjects interested him, because all of them represented what he called 'a vigorous flourish of life'.

THE GATEKEEPER

Cabbages were a vigorous flourish of life, and so was Locke's theory of essences, and so was the Crimean war. All of them had their place in the great multicoloured quilt of reality, and the point was to savour them, not go in for narrowing value judgements. All that could be left to the life-denying, petty-bourgeois puritans. He kept a volume of Lawrence Durrell's *Alexandria Quartet*, then the last word in audacious avant-gardism, lying mock-casually on his mantelpiece, no doubt to demonstrate his entirely non-existent openness to the new. One of my friends commentated dryly that before Durrell it had probably been James Joyce's *Ulysses*. He was a connoisseur of life, and when he retired from the college he actually became a wine merchant. I do not mean that he ran a slum off-licence like my father. I mean that small vans with my supervisor's name emblazoned on their side would dart around Cambridge bearing crates of vintage wine to the more opulent and discerning of the local population. In a sense he came out, publicly declaring what he had secretly been all along. For it was really as a wine merchant that he approached literature, rolling a little Tennyson on his tongue, shipping in great crates of minor seventeenth-century verse, finding George Orwell distinctly unpalatable and D. H. Lawrence rather too heady. He was occasionally a little unsteady on his feet after a prolonged bout of Ovid.

I studied the Tragedy paper in the English School with him, and we came to conceptual blows over it almost from the outset. Greenway believed that tragedy was a rare, quasi-religious ritual which could no longer exist in the modern world, whereas I thought I had excellent reason for believing that there was still more than enough of it about. Our discussions of the tragic were hobbled from the start by a fundamental disagreement: I thought tragedy was a bad thing, whereas he thought it was a good one. He would suggest to me essay titles like: 'Though Ibsen is a notably fine dramatist, his work does not quite attain the status of tragedy', as though striving for tragic status but falling short of it was rather like aspiring to play the oboe but having to fall back defeated on the tin whistle. For him, a word which meant misery and destitution was supremely positive, on a level with 'chivalry' or 'sautéd oysters'. He also assumed that tragedy was always a deeper affair than comedy, whereas I could not see how Tennessee Williams was necessarily deeper than Dante.

The real problem, however, was that Greenway's aversion to ideas made him incapable of spelling out his case, which was as instinctive as his taste in cheese. I was accordingly reduced to having to put his case for him in order to rebut it, like a ventriloquist with a disputatious dummy. This proved a fatiguing business, like trying to be one's own tennis partner. Greenway thought that it was foolish to want to live, as I did, in a society which had passed beyond tragedy, since to lose our sense of the tragic would mean losing our sense of value.

Yet he must have known what I was talking about. He knew; he was there at the time. How could he not know that I had the evidence to refute his case?

Tragedy for Greenway was largely a literary affair. Perhaps he harboured some secret wound or had suffered some gut-wrenching loss, but it seemed unlikely. The combined efforts of butler, maid, gardener, porters and college servants seemed to have swaddled him from a few of life's nastier, more Agamemnon-like knocks. Indeed, in this respect he and my Carmelites were not so different. Oxbridge colleges are something of a cross between a monastery and a four-star hotel, a strange blend of cloisters and caviar. And Greenway, though I doubt he wore chafing knickers and rose at dawn to pray, was in his own way as remote from the world of discos and baby-food as was Sister Angela. Both knew a lot about brutality and despair, but strictly at second hand. The college was at that time an all-male precinct, as the convent was an all-female one. When I first became a Fellow of an Oxford college, there was an institution known as 'wives' dinner', which was the only time one's wife was allowed to dine as a guest at High Table. But she could not be *your* guest. That would be far too drearily domestic. Instead, Fellows would indulge in a spot of ceremonial wife-swapping for the occasion, each playing host to the other's wife.

Greenway was a bachelor when I first encountered him, although already in his late forties, and appeared content with his condition; but we returned from one summer vacation to discover that he had suddenly married. It was as hard to imagine him married as it was to imagine him mud-wrestling, but we dared one another to raise the topic with him, and the student who drew the short straw had the nerve to congratulate him on the event. Greenway's response was 'It's all very interesting,' as though he was speaking of a physics experiment or a particularly enthralling account of logical positivism.

But he was not, perhaps, quite as detached from such carnal matters as it seemed. I once went along to the Cambridge Arts theatre to see a production of a Greek tragedy in which the Chorus turned out to be a set of lithe, writhing, scantily clad young women who chanted their lines in an orgasmic moan. As the moaning reached a crescendo, a faint wailing, gasping sound drifted up from the front rows of the stalls to mingle with it. The gasping turned into a convulsive fit of coughing, and I turned to see Greenway being led up the aisle by a female companion, puce-faced and bent double, overcome by what was either a fit of asthma or an erotic paroxysm.

Pain, tragedy, class, sacrifice, trauma: where do all these converge?

I was sitting in Greenway's study on my first visit to Cambridge, waiting to be interviewed for an undergraduate place. The faint braying of public-school boys could be heard through the eighteenth-century window panes, along with the plashing of the fountain where Byron used to tether his pet bear. Over my years in Oxbridge I was to hear that full-throated bray modulate gradually into more demotic mode, as the populist 60s, leftist 70s and marketeering 80s rolled by, and as the children of the well-to-do strived gamely to roughen up their vowels and derange their consonants, inserting the odd glottal stop into their speech like someone distressing a perfectly good pair of jeans.

It was only my second trip south of Watford, the first having been an abortive visit to London. I had won a scholarship to spend a week at Stratford, and had met there a young woman, a sixth-former from Surrey, who described herself to me rather earnestly as an 'eclectic'. I was unsure whether this was a religion, a geographical region, a medical disorder or a sexual tendency, but the two of us fell instantly in what had all the spurious appearances of love. I rowed her manfully on the Avon, my newly nurtured wisp of a beard quivering in the breeze, and as the swans drifted upon the darkening flood I spoke to her sombrely of the essential vacuity of human existence. Over a half-pint in the Dirty Duck she confided to me her adherence to the philosophy of D. H. Lawrence, an adherence which turned out to be a little too abstract for my taste, while I expounded to her the thought of Nietzsche, whose name I pronounced Knee-etch, and tried not to choke on a small cigar. With hands chastely interlinked, we sat in the Stratford theatre watching a twenty-seven-year-old Peter O'Toole, still fresh from the west of Ireland, perform his guttural, melancholic, austerely dignified Shylock. We arranged to spend a few days together in London, and she met me in the railway station buffet. She asked me what refreshments I would like, and I heard myself announce in my lugubrious Northern tones: 'I'll 'ave a buun.' She gave an amused tinkle of Home Counties laughter and I watched our relationship wither before my eyes. It was clearly duchess and gamekeeper stuff. She rode a horse, I rode a bike. But she was a kind, finely intelligent woman, and I later heard that she became a top civil servant. I sometimes wonder whether she ever had access to my political file.

There were two other candidates for interview waiting in Greenway's study, one a young fogey in a dark, serious suit who spoke in measured, annoyingly reasonable tones, and the other a svelte, flaxen-haired youth in a suit with flamboyantly broad stripes like a cartoon bookmaker. They were deep in conversation, though I could not tell whether they knew each other already, indeed perhaps were schoolmates, or whether people of this social background simply fell spontaneously into conversation together when they met, like victims of cystic fibrosis or Latvian immigrants in

Omaha. My bet was that the young fogey would get a place but that the svelte bookmaker would not.

The door to the inner room opened suddenly and Greenway entered. He was short and lean, though with a neat little gut which looked built in to his wine-coloured waistcoat, and his bright-eyed, hook-nosed features were those of a fastidious bird. His movements were nervous but exact. The two other youths leapt instantly to their feet, a response which struck me as somewhat uncalled for but which I thought it prudent to imitate. Greenway looked straight at me and pronounced my name in a dry rasp, though I knew that the other two candidates had alphabetical priority in being interviewed. I wondered how he knew which one of us was me, since we had not met before, unless in some scandalous outbreak of Oxbridge nepotism the other two were his nephews. Perhaps I was the one who had failed the entrance exam, though so far we had only sat two papers, one of them a relatively unimportant translation paper. Maybe he was getting me out of the way so that he could crack the champagne with the other two. It looked as though I was not destined to be a Patron after all.

Greenway led me into his inner sanctum, waved me to an armchair, and stared at me for an embarrassingly long time with his finger stuck sideways in his mouth. He was biting the finger hard as though to stop himself from screaming, and if I had not been so nervous myself I would have sworn that he was nervous too. Then he removed his finger from his mouth and said: 'My dear fellow, I have some very bad and very sad news for you.' I noted the rhyme even as I felt my stomach heave. So I had failed the exam. Had my translations really been that bad? By a stroke of luck, the unseen passage of Latin was one I had done already at school, so I thought I had tackled it rather well. But the one English paper I had taken so far might well have been below standard.

'Your father died last night. I'm so awfully sorry.' He stuck his finger back in his mouth, biting it hard with his eyes frightened and flaring, and I could see that he was terrified that I was going to scream. It was as though he was signalling that he was simply not equipped to cope with emotional outbursts, and was mutely begging me not to break down. But I felt nothing except feeling this, in a moment of anaes-thesia for which later in life I was to pay dearly. My father had been dying when I left the shop, and it was always on the cards that he would not survive my absence. We had considered whether I should stay at home until his death, or whether I should do what he wanted for me by trying for a Cambridge place. Now he had died anyway, and I had done too little of the entrance exam to get in.

Greenway asked me if I would like to phone home, and discreetly left the room. A porter came on the line to ask me superciliously whether Dr Greenway was aware that I was using his telephone. I spoke to my mother, but she was in no condition to decide whether I should come home for the funeral or stay on to finish the exam. My headmaster – a rather more humane successor to Brother Damian – then intervened and ordered me home, a decision I felt glad about in one way and sorry in another. I was tempted to stay on for the exam, but uncertain whether this would be altruism or self-interest. Would I be abandoning my father or keeping faith with him? Perhaps only by doing the first could I do the second; perhaps that was part of what he had meant.

I went home to confront the unclean, traumatic thing,

and instead confronted my headmaster at the back of the church where my father's coffin was lying. I hissed angrily that he had no right to meddle, that my father would have wanted me to stay on at Cambridge, that he was simply elevating ritual over reality in despicably papist fashion. In paying homage to my father he was destroying in his blundering, cack-handed way the very thing my father had desired. Didn't he see that I had to get away from my father in order to get away for him? The headmaster, a cleric, was soothing and imperturbable, no doubt treating my fury purely as a reflex of grief. What seemed to me ironies of the situation seemed to him the incoherencies of bereavement. I had to make a sacrifice for my father's sake, he told me, and I flashed back that this was nonsense, that to do so was to make a mockery of my father's own sacrifice. I think he thought at one point that I was going to hit him, which for my pious grandparents would probably have meant being turned into a donkey on the spot or at the very least ending up with a withered arm. Perhaps I would disappear in a cackle of demonic laughter, go up in a puff of metaphysical smoke. But I did not know whether I was fighting him, Cambridge, or my father.

Some weeks later, a letter arrived from Greenway to say that I had been awarded a place as a commoner, and regretting the fact that my failure to complete the entrance exam meant that I could be elected neither to an exhibition nor a scholarship. It was like commiserating with someone just cured of blindness that he would still have the odd touch of eye strain. I do not think that Greenway acted out of pity or compassion. He was a man for the strict equivalencies of justice, not the spendthrift gesture. My sole English paper must have been better than I imagined. Even so, his action burst on me like a strange kind of forgiveness. The gatekeeper had let me in, though it was my father who had turned the key. Greenway had accepted me as a literary type; had my father ever done as much? Perhaps this was one reason why I kicked so hard against Greenway when I got to Cambridge. His world was the Law which had brought my father to his ruin, but it was a Law which my father was asking me to love.

Greenway had taken what I suspect was one of the very few risks of his preternaturally prudent life; and though I covered him with reflected academic glory, and even gained in time the exhibition and scholarship for which I had first disqualified myself, he was later perhaps to come to regret his decision. He had nurtured a Marxist viper in his bosom, which was finally let loose upon the world to poison all that he held precious. That's where being generous to the working classes gets you. Later, while job-hunting, I was quietly advised to stop using him as a referee. His references would have been bracingly honest. But I was always thankful to him, and wrote to tell him so when he retired. He did not reply, rather perhaps as he had not left his room to greet the dying Wittgenstein.

But all that was later. We buried my father one frosty December morning, and afterwards my mother came home from the churchyard and opened the shop.